P9-CER-084

Diversity Programming and Outreach for Academic Libraries

CHANDOS
INFORMATION PROFESSIONAL SERIES

Series Editor: Ruth Rikowski
(e-mail: Rikowskigr@aol.com)

Chandos' new series of books is aimed at the busy information professional. They have been specially commissioned to provide the reader with an authoritative view of current thinking. They are designed to provide easy-to-read and (most importantly) practical coverage of topics that are of interest to librarians and other information professionals. If you would like a full listing of current and forthcoming titles, please visit our website www.chandospublishing.com or e-mail info@chandospublishing.com or telephone +44 (0) 1223 499140.

New authors: we are always pleased to receive ideas for new titles; if you would like to write a book for Chandos, please contact Dr Glyn Jones on e-mail gjones@chandospublishing. com or telephone number +44 (0) 1993 848726.

Bulk orders: some organisations buy a number of copies of our books. If you are interested in doing this, we would be pleased to discuss a discount. Please e-mail info@chandospublishing.com or telephone +44 (0) 1223 499140.

Diversity Programming and Outreach for Academic Libraries

KATHLEEN A. HANNA, MINDY M. COOPER AND ROBIN A. CRUMRIN

CP

CHANDOS
PUBLISHING

Oxford Cambridge New Delhi

Chandos Publishing
Hexagon House
Avenue 4
Station Lane
Witney
Oxford OX28 4BN
UK
Tel: +44 (0) 1993 848726
E-mail: info@chandospublishing.com
www.chandospublishing.com

Chandos Publishing is an imprint of Woodhead Publishing Limited

Woodhead Publishing Limited
80 High Street
Sawston
Cambridge CB22 3HJ
UK
Tel: +44 (0) 1223 499140
Fax: +44 (0) 1223 832819
www.woodheadpublishing.com

First published in 2011

ISBN:
978 1 84334 635 7

© K. Hanna, M. Cooper and R. Crumrin, 2011

British Library Cataloguing-in-Publication Data.
A catalogue record for this book is available from the British Library.

All rights reserved. No part of this publication may be reproduced, stored in or introduced into a retrieval system, or transmitted, in any form, or by any means (electronic, mechanical, photocopying, recording or otherwise) without the prior written permission of the Publishers. This publication may not be lent, resold, hired out or otherwise disposed of by way of trade in any form of binding or cover other than that in which it is published without the prior consent of the Publishers. Any person who does any unauthorised act in relation to this publication may be liable to criminal prosecution and civil claims for damages.

The Publishers make no representation, express or implied, with regard to the accuracy of the information contained in this publication and cannot accept any legal responsibility or liability for any errors or omissions.

The material contained in this publication constitutes general guidelines only and does not represent to be advice on any particular matter. No reader or purchaser should act on the basis of material contained in this publication without first taking professional advice appropriate to their particular circumstances. All screenshots in this publication are the copyright of the website owner(s), unless indicated otherwise.

Typeset by RefineCatch Limited, Bungay, Suffolk
Printed in the UK and USA.

Contents

Appendices

List of figures and tables

Figures

Tables

List of abbreviations

AAUP	American Association of University Professors
ACRL	Association of College and Research Libraries
AES	Adaptive Educational Services
ALA	American Library Association
ALIA	Australian Library and Information Association
CDCG	Collection Development Coordinating Group
CLA	Canadian Library Association
CNN	Cable News Network
COG	Campus Outreach Group
CTL	Center for Teaching and Learning
FIFA	Federation Internationale de Football Association
GA	Graduate Assistant
GLBT	Gay/Lesbian/Bisexual/Transgender
GPA	Grade Point Average
IFLA	International Federation of Library Associations
IMIR	Information Management and Institutional Research
INTRAA	Indiana Transgender Rights Advocacy Alliance
IUPUI	Indiana University Purdue University Indianapolis
LLID	Librarians Leading in Diversity
LSTA	Library Services and Technology Act
NACADA	National Academic Advising Association
NEH	National Endowment for the Humanities
ODEI	Office of Diversity, Equity and Inclusion

OIA	Office of International Affairs
PULs	Principles of Undergraduate Learning
RISE	Research, International, Service Learning, Experiential Learning
SLIS	School of Library and Information Science
SUNO	Southern University of New Orleans
UITS	University Information Technology Services
UL	University Library
ULFO	University Library Faculty Organization
ULSG	University Library Specialists Group
VCU	Virginia Commonwealth University

About the authors

Kathleen A. Hanna, MIS, is an Associate Librarian at Indiana University – Purdue University Indianapolis (IUPUI) and is University Library's liaison to the IUPUI School of Physical Education and Tourism Management. She served as supervisor to the 2008 – 2009 Diversity Scholars.

Mindy M. Cooper, MLS, serves as the past chair of the Diversity Council and a member of the Reference Team and Campus Outreach Group at University Library. She was named the 2008 Outstanding New Librarian by the Indiana Library Federation.

Robin A. Crumrin, MLS, served as a Diversity Scholar supervisor and Diversity Council committee member at University Library. She is the Associate Dean for Collections and Information Access Services.

Introduction to diversity in academic libraries

Abstract: This chapter discusses the trend of increased diversity in universities, both among student and faculty populations, and how diversity may be defined in the academy and, therefore, in academic libraries. It describes Indiana University-Purdue University Indianapolis (IUPUI), its campus atmosphere and demographics, and the IUPUI University Library and its staff.

Key words: Indiana University-Purdue University Indianapolis, IUPUI, diversity, multiculturalism, outreach, programming, academic libraries, Principles of Undergraduate Learning, student code of conduct, American Library Association (ALA), Canadian Library Association (CLA), Australian Library and Information Association (ALIA), International Federation of Library Associations (IFLA).

Definitions

Diversity, or at the minimum, a statement about commitment to diversity, is becoming a common thread among universities and colleges. How can academic libraries put action and conviction behind broad and sometimes lofty definitions? How might we embrace our differences and unify our services for a diverse population?

By our definition diversity includes, but is not limited to, various related attributes:

- ability

- age

- cultural heritage

- ethnic background

- gender

- gender identity

- national origin

- race

- religion

- sexual orientation

- socio-economic status.

The goal at our library, Indiana University-Purdue University, Indianapolis (IUPUI) University Library, is to promote a positive work and learning environment free from any form of bigotry, harassment, intimidation, threat, or abuse, whether verbal or written, physical or psychological, direct or implied.

In defining outreach in this book, we refer to academic libraries going beyond providing normal user services, such as reference and research assistance or collection development, and creating additional staff functions that are focused on the library 'making contact and fostering relations with people unconnected with it, esp[ecially] for the purpose of support or education and for increasing awareness of the organization's aims or message' (*Oxford English Dictionary Online*).

We characterize programming here as special events that have been initiated and developed by library staff specifically to engage students and that foster awareness and understanding of diverse populations.

Indiana University-Purdue University Indianapolis (IUPUI)

In 1969, IUPUI was formed as a partnership between Indiana University and Purdue University, an effort to bring together Indiana University and Purdue University schools existing in different areas in Indianapolis. IUPUI is one of the top five 'up and coming' American universities that *U.S. News and World Report* says people should be watching, and the 8th best public college in the Midwest according to *Forbes* magazine. IUPUI is home to nationally-ranked programs in nursing, public and environmental affairs, law, and health; and is a campus renowned for service learning and civic engagement. IUPUI encompasses 20 schools and academic units granting degrees in more than 200 programs from both Indiana University and Purdue University.

IUPUI enrolls approximately 30,000 students representing all 50 states and 122 countries. The highest percentages of our international students are from China, India, Saudi Arabia, South Korea, and Taiwan. The majority of our international students are pursuing degrees in the Schools of Engineering and Technology, Science, Business, and Medicine. Through campus surveys administered by IUPUI's Information Management & Institutional Research (IMIR) unit, our international students also report fairly high satisfaction rates (approximately 85 percent) with the libraries at IUPUI, although there is obviously still room for improvement.

Indiana University and IUPUI have made public and specific written commitments embracing diversity. The Indiana University Board of Trustees statement of the University's Objectives and Ideals states, in part, that 'Indiana University is committed to the principle of equal educational and occupational opportunities for all persons and to positive action toward elimination of discrimination in all phases of University life, as set forth in the Indiana University Affirmative Action Plan' (June 29, 1974; Indiana University Academic Handbook, 1992, p. 2, Appendix F). In the IUPUI Supplement to the IU Academic Handbook (Appendix G), the IUPUI administration clearly states the expectations for this campus: 'As an institution of higher learning, we have a special obligation to not only follow the letter of the laws that protect our individual rights and human dignity but also to champion the spirit of the laws. Periodically, we must reaffirm the fundamental ethics and values that form the groundwork for the university climate we wish to maintain. Among those values is fostering a climate of civility and mutual respect regardless of race, gender, age or status in the institution. Our institutional ethic demands that we foster the best possible environment for doing our work as educators, learners, and supporters of the educational process' (Indiana University Academic Handbook IUPUI Supplement 95–97, p. 57).

IUPUI also embeds its commitment to multiculturalism and diversity in the curriculum through its renowned Principles of Undergraduate Learning (PULs) (*http://faa .iupui.edu/pul/*), particularly the fifth PUL:

> Understanding Society and Culture: The ability of students to recognize their own cultural traditions and to understand and appreciate the diversity of the human experience.
>
> Understanding society and culture is demonstrated by the student's ability to:
>
> 1. compare and contrast the range of diversity and universality in human history, societies, and ways of life;

2. analyze and understand the interconnectedness of global and local communities; and

3. operate with civility in a complex world.

The university has also included wording in the Code of Student Rights, Responsibilities and conduct [*http://www .iupui.edu/code/*] to underscore its commitment:

> Students have the right to study, work, and interact in an environment that is free from discrimination in violation of law or university policy by any member of the university community. Students at Indiana University are expected to respect the rights and dignity of other students, faculty, and staff.
>
> The university will not exclude any person from participation in its programs or activities on the basis of arbitrary considerations of such characteristics as age, color, disability, ethnicity, sex or gender, marital status, national origin, race, religion, sexual orientation, or veteran status.
>
> A student has the right to be free from such discrimination by other students that has the effect of interfering with the student's ability to participate in programs or activities of the university.
>
> (Section I.B. 'Right to Freedom from Discrimination')

Students must 'respect the rights and dignity of others both within and outside of the university community' and are advised of the consequences for harassment, implied threats, and verbal or physical abuse of others.

Figures 1.1 and 1.2 below illustrate the breakdown of minorities and women students, faculty, and staff at IUPUI. Student counts are divided by undergraduate (UG) and graduate (Grad/Prof.) level enrollments. IUPUI tracks the

Figure 1.1   Student enrollment trend: IUPUI Indianapolis only

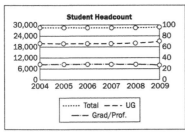

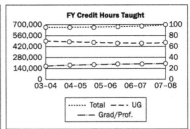

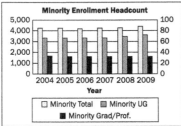

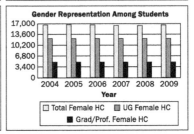

Figure 1.2   Faculty and staff headcount: IUPUI Indianapolis only

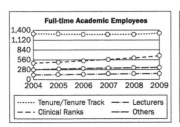

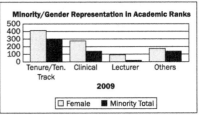

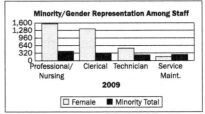

following US ethnic minority groups: African American, Asian/Pacific Islander, Hispanic/Latino, and Native American. International students are counted separately (courtesy of IUPUI Information Management & Institutional Research, *http://imir.iupui.edu/*).

Table 1.1 illustrates international student satisfaction with the University Library (courtesy of IUPUI Information Management & Institutional Research 2009 International Student Barometer Survey, *http://imir.iupui.edu/surveys/ reports/default.aspx/OTH/OTH_ISB/65/3/2009*).

As a relatively young and urban campus, IUPUI has witnessed a great influx of diverse student and faculty populations. Our enrollment of international students more than doubled from 1999 to 2008 (*http://www.iport.iupui .edu/iupui/statportrait/data.aspx*). In addition, IUPUI currently has formal partnerships with three major universities: Sun Yat-Sen University (Guangdong Province, China), Moi University (Eldoret, Kenya), and Universidad Autónoma del Estado de Hidalgo (Pachuca Hidalgo, Mexico).

Students at IUPUI have access to scores of established study-abroad programs through the Big Ten schools consortium (*http://www.cic.net/*), Indiana University-Bloomington, and at School and department levels, such as summer art history studies in Guanajuato, Mexico (through partner University of Iowa), year-long multi-disciplinary courses in Freiberg, Germany (through Indiana University-Bloomington), central and eastern European law studies in Mlini, Croatia (IUPUI program), and two- or three-month internships in Istanbul, Turkey (for students of the School of Engineering and Technology).

Beyond cultural and ethnic considerations, IUPUI is home to a coeducational student population of wide-ranging ages, abilities, socio-economic backgrounds, gender identities/ sexual orientations, and religions. It is not unusual for young

Table 1.1 University breakdown – entry wave 2009: Indiana U-Purdue U Indianapolis

	Base (Overall Satisfaction)	675		28	647	157	124	104	51	37
ISB	LEARNING SATISFACTION									
		Satisfaction		Region		Nationality				
Importance	Learning elements	ISB	IUPUI	EU	Non-EU	China	India	Saudi Ara	South Kor	Taiwan
97%	Good teachers	86%	87%	96%	86%	88%	84%	79%	87%	96%
97%	Course content	88%	87%	96%	86%	91%	74%	84%	90%	100%
97%	Expert lecturers	94%	91%	100%	91%	92%	95%	85%	83%	96%
95%	Assessment	86%	90%	96%	90%	93%	86%	84%	82%	93%
93%	Library	85%	87%	100%	86%	89%	86%	90%	69%	85%
93%	Technology	86%	90%	84%	91%	91%	97%	86%	82%	93%
93%	Performance feedback	83%	87%	92%	86%	92%	88%	78%	77%	89%
89%	Employability	77%	73%	76%	72%	75%	69%	79%	58%	78%
93%	Learning support	83%	86%	83%	87%	92%	86%	81%	74%	100%
91%	Flexibility	83%	84%	92%	84%	92%	81%	78%	71%	89%
86%	Academics' English	89%	91%	91%	91%	92%	95%	90%	87%	93%
84%	Work experience	66%	66%	75%	66%	73%	62%	69%	51%	72%
84%	Careers advice	67%	68%	75%	68%	75%	67%	76%	45%	67%
85%	Research	87%	84%	96%	83%	90%	78%	83%	70%	89%
86%	Learning spaces	84%	87%	96%	87%	89%	92%	81%	68%	93%
75%	Language support	82%	82%	85%	82%	80%	88%	76%	68%	78%
74%	Opportunities to teach	71%	76%	67%	76%	78%	71%	80%	33%	67%
76%	Multicultural	87%	84%	88%	83%	80%	87%	78%	80%	81%

students arriving straight from high school to share their classrooms with single parents, returning military veterans, and middle-aged adults, or for faculty to adjust their pedagogy for multiple learning styles or students' life experiences, online or hybrid courses, or to account for a lack of student access to technology at home. To support students of disparate abilities and socio-economic backgrounds, particularly those who may be first-generation scholars, the campus provides services for the physically and learning disabled (Adaptive Educational Services), learning centers for students requiring computer skills and mathematics, writing, chemistry and biology tutoring, plus numerous scholarship and on-campus employment opportunities.

IUPUI also provides meeting space and event funding for nearly 400 diverse student organizations, such as:

- Black Student Union
- Chinese Culture Club
- Achieving Disability Access and Awareness
- Muslim Alliance of Indiana Student Group
- Students Advocating for Sexuality Understanding and Equality
- Jewish Student Association
- SGI Buddhist Association
- Student Veterans at IUPUI
- Sustainable Health and Nutrition Club.

These students, and the diverse faculty population who serve them, bring to our campus varied expectations, life experiences, study and research habits, points of view, opinions, and knowledge.

For many of these students the university is often the only place where they are exposed to diverse populations and points of view and, while immersed in higher education, have the freedom to experiment with new ideas and ways of thinking. The university library can be a 'safe haven' – neutral territory that can serve as a gathering place and incubator for exploring diversity issues on campus.

IUPUI University Library

Serving as a centerpiece for the IUPUI library system the University Library, containing 1.5 million volumes, provides academic and community patrons with multiple study and learning spaces. The five-story facility also houses staff offices, study carrels, group study rooms and areas, multimedia classrooms, and a 100-seat auditorium. We provide office space for several key campus units: School of Library and Information Science (SLIS), Honors College, Center for Teaching and Learning, Center for Research and Learning, University Writing Center, and Adaptive Educational Services Learning Center. We provide services to university students, faculty and staff, as well as individual citizens, businesses, professional firms, and public agencies. University Library is the primary undergraduate library at IUPUI, with additional libraries in place to support the professional schools: Herron Art Library, Ruth Lilly Law Library, IU School of Dentistry Library, and IU School of Medicine Library. The libraries' holdings are accessed through a computer network linking Indiana University libraries state-wide, and an interlibrary loan system makes additional local, state and national academic library resources available. Over 300 public computer workstations are available in the library for our users and electronic resources may also be accessed from off campus by our students, faculty, and staff.

The vision of University Library is to:

- INFORM the IUPUI campus and wider community of learners through our educational resources, technologies, and expertise;

- CONNECT people with our resources, our services and each other;

- TRANSFORM the lives of our community members by facilitating discovery, creativity, teaching, learning and research. University Library actively partners in the transformation of information to new and more accessible formats.

Diversity in the academy

The internationalization or globalization of universities worldwide is well documented by Welch (1997), Altbach (2000), van der Wende (2001), Bartell (2003), Lee (2008), Horta (2009), Crossman and Clarke (2010), and many others. Due to the increasing globalization of economies and ease of travel and communication there is a growing interest in international student exchange. Although formal programs have existed for decades or longer, more and more universities exhibit culturally and ethnically diverse student and faculty populations. Faculty are willing to relocate for research opportunities that will enrich their careers and students for new experiences that enable them to realise their personal goals. Research, revenue, and reputation are generally excellent motivators for university administrators to recruit and retain a diverse faculty and student population.

The degree of diversity at universities varies greatly by country and institution. For some, an influx of ethnic minorities or students over the age of 25 is novel for them;

for others, women are the leaders in breaking barriers to what have formerly been all-male courses of study. What is certain however is that increasing diversity in universities is a worldwide phenomenon. An informal search of university websites indicates that institutions as varied as Australian National University, Qatar University, University of Belgrade, University of Cape Town, University of Costa Rica, University of Oxford, and University of Tokyo all support programs for international students and services for the disabled. Additionally, a casual survey of university student organizations and clubs on campuses throughout the globe, and perhaps in particular in the United States, indicates populations inclusive of varied cultural and religious backgrounds, women, gay/lesbian/bisexual/transgender (GLBT) students, a wide range of socio-political viewpoints, and the usual sports and academic interests.

Perhaps most interesting is the striking similarities in the design and content of the library websites of our sister institutions; we indeed all share common goals as well as common challenges in delivering resources and services!

Diversity in libraries

While diversity may be a fairly new concept to some universities, library associations and federations have long centered the work of their members on the belief that a library's purpose is to provide materials and services to all members of the community it serves. This belief is conveyed in mission and vision statements that guide the work of librarians around the world on a daily basis. In the United States, libraries are guided by the American Library Association's (ALA) Bill of Rights (*http://www.ala.org/ ala/issuesadvocacy/intfreedom/librarybill/index.cfm*). First adopted in 1939, the ALA Bill of Rights contains six key policies, four of which relate to the issue of diversity:

- Books and other library resources should be provided for the interest, information, and enlightenment of all people of the community the library serves. Materials should not be excluded because of the origin, background, or views of those contributing to their creation.

- Libraries should provide materials and information presenting all points of view on current and historical issues. Materials should not be proscribed or removed because of partisan or doctrinal disapproval.

- A person's right to use a library should not be denied or abridged because of origin, age, background, or views.

- Libraries which make exhibit spaces and meeting rooms available to the public they serve should make such facilities available on an equitable basis, regardless of the beliefs or affiliations of individuals or groups requesting their use.

American libraries are scarcely alone in this; among the core values of the Australian Library and Information Association (ALIA) is 'respect for the diversity and individuality of all people' (*http://www.alia.org.au/governance/alia.vision.html*) along with specific policies regarding libraries' responsibilities towards indigenous peoples (*http://www.alia.org.au/policies/aboriginal.html*) and those with disabilities (*http://www.alia.org.au/policies/disabilities.html*). These policy statements call for librarians to be involved in planning, advocacy and cooperation with other agencies in providing the best possible library services and resources to these groups.

Canadian librarians express the belief that diversity is important by their association's value statement that 'libraries and the principles of intellectual freedom and free universal access to information are key components of an open and democratic society'. But they further stress the importance of diversity by stating that 'diversity is a major strength' of their organization (*http://www.cla.ca/AM/ Template.cfm?Section—Mission_Values_andamp_ Operating_Principles&Template=/CM/HTMLDisplay .cfm&ContentID=8621*).

The diversity of the library workforce is an important principle found in the International Federation of Library Associations and Institutions (IFLA) Multicultural Library Manifesto (*http://archive.ifla.org/VII/s32/pub/Multicultural LibraryManifesto.pdf*). This manifesto states that to address diversity, both cultural and linguistic, all 'libraries should employ staff to reflect the diversity of the community who are trained to work with and serve diverse communities'.

The inclusion of diversity as an important principle in mission statements and guiding documents on the national and international level serves as an excellent reminder for individual librarians to be mindful of diversity issues in their work in collection development, reference services, and bibliographic instruction. In order to support intellectual freedom, librarians must provide a balanced collection to ensure all points of view are represented. When available and appropriate, materials should be collected in numerous languages and formats, both electronic and print, with standard and large type. In providing reference assistance and information literacy instruction, library staff must be cognizant of the diversity of its user population. Challenges in some situations may be obvious – helping a student who is visually impaired, in a wheelchair, or not a native speaker, may cause library staff to adjust how they deliver information. Helms (1998) points out a few concepts to think about that might not be obvious to library staff: the concept of personal space, eye contact and non-verbal communication. Library staff must have an understanding of cultural differences in regard to these concepts so as not to offend others and to give the best service possible. They should also be aware of the diversity of learning styles and less apparent learning disabilities and be prepared to alter their approaches accordingly.

Diversity outreach and programming in international academic libraries

Although diversity in universities worldwide has been widely acknowledged, and the IFLA stresses the growing need to provide services to multicultural populations, we have been unable to locate diversity outreach and programming in academic libraries as defined on page 2 of this chapter beyond a small number of institutions in the United States. We have performed literature searches and perused many university library websites in numerous countries. We assume our inability to locate other academic libraries doing similar outreach and programming may be due to a combination of factors: we simply did not look in all the right places, similar initiatives are described in different terms, language barriers prevented us from properly identifying appropriate areas on foreign-language websites, and we lacked sufficient knowledge and familiarity with the nature and traditions of academic libraries in other countries.

If our colleagues in academic libraries outside the United States are engaged in diversity outreach and programming as defined above, we hope they will celebrate their efforts so we may learn from each other and continue to expand upon these exciting and rewarding endeavors.

In the following chapters, we will explore what we have accomplished to date at IUPUI University Library in the hope that what we have done can be adapted or adopted by others interested in developing their own diversity initiatives.

2

Creating a Diversity Council

Abstract: This chapter discusses how IUPUI reaffirmed its commitment to diversity following a report submitted by a student organization. The resulting mandate to campus units prompted IUPUI University Library to not only create its Diversity Council to oversee all diversity-related library initiatives, but to challenge itself and the library to exceed the campus administration's expectations.

Key words: diversity council, charter, mission statement, strategic plan, university library, IUPUI, Black Student Union, diversity cabinet, Yale University, Georgia State University.

Call for diversity as a priority at IUPUI

As discussed in the previous chapter, the work of academic librarians, including those at IUPUI University Library, is often centered on diversity. But on November 2, 2006, all academic units on the IUPUI campus became more aware of diversity issues after the Black Student Union released 'Through Our Eyes: The State of the Black Student at Indiana University-Purdue University Indianapolis' (*http://diversity.iupui.edu/assets/061102_through_our_eyes.pdf*). In this report, the students noted several grievances against the university, including:

- IUPUI officials do not communicate effectively with the Black student population.
- There is not enough black programming on the IUPUI campus, facilitated by the University, as they do other groups. Furthermore, black student organizations do more programming on this campus than any other organization and we are not recognized for this.
- There is a lack of equity and true cultural competence for the Black student population.
- IUPUI does not allot funding as they should to Black Student Organizations.

The students advocated improved communication, acceptance and respect, multi-faceted support for black students, cultural competencies embedded in the curricula, and increased funding for the Black Student Union. The report was also widely disseminated to the local media. In response to 'Through Our Eyes' and intense discussions at two campus town hall meetings that followed in early 2007, the University's administration devised an action plan that called for the appointment of a full-time IUPUI diversity officer, mechanisms to provide equitable funding for all student organizations, and a promise to create a campus Multicultural Center (*http://mc.iupui.edu/*). Although the university had conducted campus diversity surveys since 1999 and in 2003 formed the Chancellor's Diversity Cabinet (composed of administrators, faculty, staff, and student representatives), the Black Student Union's bold and honest report was a sobering reminder of the work still to do on our campus. In 2008, the Office of Diversity, Equity, & Inclusion (ODEI) was created, headed by the new Assistant Chancellor of Diversity.

Additionally, each academic unit was charged with organizing its own diversity committee or cabinet and devising a strategic plan that would help the campus with its IUPUI Campus Diversity Goals, including:

- Recruitment, academic achievement, persistence and graduation of a diverse student body;

- Recruit, retain, advance, recognize, and promote a diverse faculty, staff and administration while creating a campus-wide community that celebrates its own diversity as one of its strengths and as a means of shaping IUPUI's identity as a university;

- Make diversity a strategic priority touching all aspects of the campus mission;

- Regularly assess, evaluate, improve, and communicate diversity efforts of IUPUI.

> From Vision, Mission and Goals of the University:
> Office of Diversity, Equity & Inclusion
> (*http://diversity.iupui.edu/vision.html*)

The libraries are mentioned specifically in the goals on the website noted above, but only to the extent that it provides books and other resources: 'Maintain and enhance the library collections that reflect the full diversity of the human experience and commentary on it, and resist censorship or restriction of access to scholarly materials' (Curricular and Co-Curricular Transformation, Goal 1.D.). As observed in the previous chapter, libraries already have, of course, been doing this for quite some time.

Development of the IUPUI University Library Diversity Council

In early 2007, University Library formed its Diversity Council, made up of librarians, support staff, and student employees.

We hoped we could make a difference to the campus, our library, and to the profession by somehow going beyond the campus mandate – by finding ways to truly engage the IUPUI students and providing opportunities that other campus units could not. We knew our staff would be our greatest asset in achieving this as many had indicated a passion for diversity issues and were looking for ways to improve student interactions. Librarians often work with international students and can provide insight into the challenges faced by these students, from language barriers to cultural differences. But we knew that finding student employee representation, either undergraduate or graduate students, would be a challenge, given their course loads and work schedules.

All Council members were initially volunteers; later, it was decided that librarians should be elected by our internal professional association, University Library Faculty Organization (ULFO) and staff representatives by the University Library Specialist Group (ULSG). The Chair and Secretary are elected by the Council membership at the first meeting of the year. One of the first tasks for this newly created group was to consider our mission statement, charter, and strategic plan.

Literature searches were performed as a pre-planning step for initial Council meetings and these revealed several helpful sources for developing our strategy, including an American Association of University Professors (AAUP) *Academe Online* article by Grant Ingle (2005), 'Will Your Campus Diversity Initiative Work?' (*http://www.aaup.org/AAUP/pubsres/academe/2005/SO/Feat/ingl.htm*). Although we were not planning the campus initiative itself, we thought several points were appropriate for our efforts:

- The initiative has an explicit goal or set of goals.
- The initiative is driven by a recurring cycle of assessment.

- [L]eadership is committed to devoting the staff and financial resources necessary to implement recommendations emerging from the change process.

- The terminology surrounding the diversity effort is unambiguous.

- The initiative has unambiguous support from campus leaders but is not dependent on any one of them.

Georgia State University's '2001–2002 Best Practices in Diversity Report' (*http://www.gsu.edu/oddep/30812.html*) also offered some excellent insights.

We based our documents primarily on the 'Yale University Library Strategic Plan for Diversity 2006–2008'. At the time, it was one of the few US academic libraries with a well-developed diversity initiative that we were able to locate by Internet search. These and other factors shaped our documents and influenced our direction. Current documents may be viewed online – 'IUPUI University Library Strategic Plan for Diversity 2007–2009' (*http://www.ulib.iupui.edu/about/diversity/goals*) and 'IUPUI University Library Diversity Council Charter' (*http://www.ulib.iupui.edu/about/diversity/plan*) (see Appendix A).

With a charter and membership in place, we needed to determine our objectives and what actions needed to take place to allow the library to support the campus goals. The Council felt that the next step was to investigate IUPUI's demographics and those of the library's staff, if possible. Being a public university, IUPUI is fortunate that the Office of Information Management and Institutional Research (IMIR) [*http://www.imir.iupui.edu/*] makes such statistics publicly available on its website. Other libraries may need to play detective by contacting the admissions or enrollment department, or some other office that serves as the clearing house for information gathered about students. If demographic information is not readily available, librarians should consider preparing a survey to gather this important information about the patrons they serve. Unfortunately, the university is unable to compile statistics on all aspects of diversity as defined in the previous chapter, due to a need to protect privacy. For example, we have no clear idea of the size of our populations of students, faculty, and staff with disabilities (physical/mental disabilities or learning disabilities), various gender identities and sexual orientations, or religions. The variety and number of our campus student organizations may be our best indicator of the current state of these diverse populations (*http://life .iupui.edu/osi/student-orgs/*).

University Library discovered that it is hardly a microcosm of the university, at least as far as representing diverse ethnicities. We have staff members who have been at University Library for over 25 years and student workers recently graduated from high school, therefore representing a wide range of ages. We have a mix of differing socio-economic backgrounds, religious and ideological viewpoints, and sexual orientations. Few minorities or people of varied ethnic origins are employed as librarians or staff, although our staff is enriched by many of our part-time student employees who are international students. By necessity, a large percentage of our part-time student workers are graduate students in the School of Library and Information Science and we were already aware of the lack of diversity in the profession and the difficulties in recruiting more diverse students. This, too, helped shape our goal to find ways to nurture a more diverse staff.

We also realized we needed a stable, dedicated online workspace for the Council. Our in-house technical staff set up an internal e-mail listserv and shared space on a computer server to facilitate communications and give us a place to store documents and records, such as meeting minutes. Public web pages were developed by the Council's Secretary and placed on the library's website.

In the three years since the Council was created, we have discovered that it is the shepherding of documents into the shared online space that may be one of the most challenging aspects of conducting Council business. In compiling information for this book, we realized we could have better captured some details and nuances of planning, projects, events, and other aspects of the Council's activities and anticipated the need for a repository to document the student work which grew out of the Council's goals. We are fortunate to have access to more than adequate online storage and can house a full archive of our activities.

One of the most important goals of the Diversity Council was the creation of the University Library Undergraduate Diversity Scholar Program, which is detailed in the following chapter.

3

Institutionalizing student involvement in library initiatives

Abstract: This chapter discusses the development of the library's student advisory group and the IUPUI University Library Undergraduate Diversity Scholar Program, which may serve as a model for creating a permanent method of ensuring student input for library diversity initiatives.

Key words: student advisory group, diversity council, undergraduate diversity scholar, fellowship, student employees.

Student advisory groups

Student advisory groups have been a tried and true method of receiving input from academic libraries' primary users and keeping fingers on the campus pulse. University Library formed its first formal student advisory group in 2009 as an outgrowth of the Campus Outreach Group (COG), a marketing and outreach committee composed of library faculty. COG librarians placed a call for student representatives on the library's website and contacted the Undergraduate Student Government and Graduate Student Organization for their assistance with recruiting from within student organizations. The library asked students to:

- Provide feedback about University Library services and collection
- Promote University Library services and collections
- Generate library programming ideas
- Preview and evaluate proposed new services and resources
- Provide a student voice to library administration.

The student advisory group was slow to take shape, but eventually grew from two to eight students by the end of the 2009–2010 academic year. The final composition of the student group was two graduate students and six undergraduates, with a representative mix of majors from across the campus. The group contained international students but its primary focus was not on diversity, although suggestions for diversity programming were certainly not discouraged, and we were pleased that students from diverse populations wished to serve on the student advisory group. The group continues to evolve and it is proving to be a valuable tool in gathering student input on a variety of issues, many of which the library is only beginning to explore. For example, the library sought and received input from the student advisory group on a new area in the reference room that will be an informal 'browsing' collection of popular fiction, magazines, music, and movies with soft seating for lounging and relaxing. At this writing, renovations have been completed and this space is now open for student's use.

Challenges to forming a student advisory group

Recruitment is the greatest challenge, of course, due to the many demands on a busy student's schedule and getting the word out takes time and commitment. The advice from the librarian leading the student advisory group is to be persistent and patient; she discovered that having regularly scheduled meetings with specific agendas gave the group purpose and moved issues forward expeditiously. Occasionally, maintaining communication was difficult – e-mail seemed to be a quick, acceptable method in a pinch – but face-to-face meetings were preferred by all. The librarian leading the student advisory group had also not anticipated that Friday meetings were problematic for Islamic students and plans in future to be more aware of cultural considerations.

Another challenge was that the students brought up ideas or issues that could not be dealt with by the group as they lacked authority to institute policy change (the librarian passed these along to appropriate library teams and departments) or were currently impractical to implement, at least from the organization's viewpoint, such as a proposal for a 24/7 accessible study area. Physical limitations of the facility, costs of staffing, and security concerns inherent in an urban campus setting were deemed prohibitive to a 24/7 space; however, a compromise was reached by extending hours until 2am during final exams week and, due to added requests by student government and other organizations, as well as financial support from the campus administration, overall library hours have been extended during fall and spring semesters. The student advisory group were pleased that their voices had been heard and action had been taken.

Rationale behind the University Library Undergraduate Diversity Scholar Program

IUPUI University Library and its newly formed Diversity Council developed a program with the intent of engaging and attracting student input to support its goal 'to create an atmosphere that is supportive of diverse populations and scholarly activity reflecting diverse populations'.

At the time, late 2006 and early 2007, emphasis was placed on introducing undergraduates to librarianship as a career. The idea was to recruit undergraduates, minorities or those interested in pursuing diversity issues, into a work environment that exposed them to librarians, the profession, and to the wealth of resources available through the library. The library has a well-established Graduate Assistantship program in collaboration with the School of Library and Information Science (SLIS) in which the Graduate Assistants (GAs) work at our Reference Desk and learn to perform other tasks, such as interlibrary loan, document digitization, and online research guide development. In order to avoid competition with SLIS GAs, this program needed to recruit undergraduates who may not have yet settled on a career and give them an opportunity to work in the library. We would then help them develop programs and events targeting the diversity found in the student population, and to hopefully attract them to the field of librarianship. Additional details about the birth of the Diversity Undergraduate Fellowship (later renamed the University Library Undergraduate Diversity Scholar Program) may be found in Hollingsworth (2008).

The foundation of the Undergraduate Diversity Scholar Program rests on the research conducted by Mary J. Stanley, Librarian Emeritus, IUPUI University Library. Ms. Stanley developed focus groups, working with the Campus and Community Life Office. Student organizations were more easily identified with the assistance of that office. Students from the Latino Student Association and the Black Student Union were invited to participate. Additional participants were recruited from library student workers and staff.

Among the themes that emerged from the focus groups were 'better marketing to minorities, informing students about the career at an earlier age, and highlighting the different aspects and opportunities of the field' (Stanley, 2007). The literature points to several methods of gathering input. Among these are focus groups (Stanley, 2007) and surveys. Surveys have been used in assessment but also in determining cultural climate and devising services and outreach to diverse student populations (Royse et al., 2006; Kyrillidou et al., 2009; Walter, 2005). The development of the University Library program rested on input gathered from Stanley's focus groups, reviews of the literature, and comparison of other university initiatives across the country.

The successful launch of the inaugural Undergraduate Diversity Scholar Program was recorded in the Diversity Council's 2008 annual report and included the following goals:

- Increase the diversity of the University Library Staff
- Hire individuals with a commitment to and belief in the positive effects of diversity in the workplace
- Give undergraduates the opportunity for professional level work in a library setting, providing insight into a career that may not have otherwise been considered
- Endow undergraduates with skills transferrable to any career.

It was highlighted in the report that the Program was considered to be a significant accomplishment 'with evidence of impact demonstrated through an Institute for Museum and Library Services grant that was applied for by the Indiana State Library'. The Indiana State Library had received a $1million Laura Bush 21st Century Librarian Program grant, having based a significant portion of its proposal on the University Library Diversity Scholar Program's goals and structure. The Indiana State Library's grant summary stated:

> The Indiana State Library will increase the level of ethnic diversity in all types of libraries across the state by recruiting and providing scholarships for 30 Masters of Library Science students from racially and ethnically diverse backgrounds, who will then commit to work in an Indiana Library for at least two years. Scholarship recipients will also benefit from participation in state and regional library associations, as well as other supplementary activities including special orientation meetings in various types of library settings, meetings with library directors, diversity and ethics workshops, transition to work programs, online and face-to-face support networks, and other special projects.

The result of this 2008 grant was Indiana's Librarians Leading in Diversity (LLID) program (*http://www.slis .indiana.edu/news/story.php?story_id=1794*). One of the LLID fellowship recipients who graduated with his MLS degree in summer 2010 recently received his appointment as an assistant librarian at IUPUI University Library.

Developing the Diversity Scholar Program

It is important that the program be mission or goal driven. The program should not be established without purpose in mind. In our case, we established the Undergraduate Diversity Scholar Program as an outgrowth of the Council's Diversity Goal 1: Recruitment, academic achievement, persistence and graduation of a diverse student body.

Critical to the success of any program is support of library administration and funding. The Dean of the Library established a budget line for two hourly wage positions for the Scholars. Funds for events, materials, equipment and other incidentals were authorized as needed by the Dean. The Office of Diversity, Equity and Inclusion as well as library donors also contributed funding to further the work of the Scholars.

Volunteers from the Diversity Council or library staff served as supervisors during the initial years of the program. It was decided that a librarian (or librarians) should be designated as supervisors since a goal of the program was to introduce underrepresented populations to librarianship [see Appendix C for complete Supervisor description]. With this goal in mind, the Council felt flexibility in the students' assignments would cultivate creativity as well as a sense of ownership by the Scholars in the development of their individual projects. We eventually discovered that a variety of assignments provided ongoing tasks to focus on during the Scholars' initial months of employment as they learned about the library, came to know the personnel, and planned their projects for the coming academic year.

The Diversity Council determined the duties of the Scholars might include:

- Working with digital archives, digital collections and the institutional repository;
- Creating metadata for the digital projects;
- Learning software tools (graphics, digital publishing and archiving);
- Creating exhibits for display cases and websites;
- Interacting with student groups regarding library and research related issues;

- Raising funds, grant and proposal writing;
- Blog posting and website publishing;
- Recording and transcribing oral histories;
- Designing and printing posters;
- Organizing and facilitating discussion series;
- Organizing diversity-related lecture series;
- Researching using primary materials;
- Shadowing reference desk staff;
- Interviewing library subject specialists and learning about all library departments.

The Council devised a simple application form, requesting basic information and a brief essay describing the applicant's interest in diversity and how they envision their contribution through the Scholar Program. Two recommendations were also required; most applicants provided these from past or current professors. The applications and information about the Program were posted on the library's website.

Advertising the Program

We explored various venues to advertise the Undergraduate Diversity Scholar Program, with online media becoming our preferred and most pervasive strategy. Facebook, the library's website, e-mail listservs, and the campus online newsletter all provided vehicles to spread the news and invite participation. We also utilized traditional print advertising, including pamphlets, brief advertisements in the student newspaper, flyers, and posters. By the second year of the Undergraduate Diversity Program, we found that word-of-mouth about the program generated greater interest

Figure 3.1 | Example of Diversity Scholar Program Application and Recommendation Forms

---

University Library Undergraduate Diversity Scholar Program Information 2010–2011

Requirements:
- Minimum GPA of 2.0 on a four-point scale
- Completed application packet (Please see checklist below)

Selection Criteria:
The following factors will be considered in our new Scholar: awareness of and commitment to diversity issues, community involvement, good communication skills, ability to work well in a team environment, and academic achievement.

Applicants from underrepresented populations are highly encouraged to apply.

Application Checklist:
1. Completed application (Please see next page)
2. Essay (Please see next page)
3. Two recommendations from persons to whom you are not related, such as a previous or current employer or previous or current teacher. Recommendation forms are available from the library's website at http://www.ulib.iupui.edu/about/diversity/fellowship and should be sent by the recommender via mail, fax, or email to Kathleen Hanna using the contact information below.

Submission Process:
If applicants would like to submit hard copies of their application, they should print this form and their essay and send to the address or fax number listed below:

Kathleen A. Hanna
IUPUI University Library
755 W. Michigan Street
Indianapolis, IN 46202
Fax: (317) 274-7133, Attn: Kathleen Hanna

If applicants wish to submit their applications electronically, they should complete and save this form, then attach this file and their essay file to the following email address: kgreatba@iupui.edu.

Deadline:
All applications should be received no later than 5:00pm on Friday, April 2, 2010

Note: As a part-time employee of IUPUI, you will be required to agree to a background check before final offer of the Scholar's position.

Figure 3.1 Example of Diversity Scholar Program Application and Recommendation Forms *(Cont'd)*

**University Library Undergraduate Diversity Scholar Program
Application 2010–2011**

Personal Information

Name:

Address:

City, State Zip:

Phone Number:

Campus E-mail:

Student ID Number:

Academic Information

School(s) attended:

GPA (on a 4.0 scale):

Other Relevant Information

List the activities in which you have been most involved, including but not limited to service activities in your community, school, or religious institution:

List any previous work experience:

Essay

In 500 words or less, discuss what you believe are the benefits of a multi-ethnic, multicultural, and diverse society, and how your activities allow you to contribute to such an environment. Please attach essay on separate sheet.

Figure 3.1   Example of Diversity Scholar Program Application and Recommendation Forms *(Cont'd)*

University Library Undergraduate Diversity Scholar Recommendation Form 2010–2011

You have been asked to recommend a student for the University Library Diversity Undergraduate Scholar Program. For more information, please visit the library's website at: *http://www.ulib.iupui.edu/about/diversity/fellowship*

Student Name:

Recommendation:

I have known the applicant for ___ years in my capacity as _____.

Please rate the applicant on each of the following characteristics in comparison with others at the same level by checking the box next to the appropriate number (1 = weak; 5 = exceptional).

	1	2	3	4	5
Dependability, reliability					
Communication skills					
Ability to work well as part of a team					
Organizational skills					
Ability to work independently					
Problem-solving skills					

Please provide your candid assessment of why you believe the applicant will be successful in a team-oriented work environment. Additionally, tell us why you believe the applicant's skills will help promote multicultural awareness at University Library. Please cite specific examples to support your recommendation. If necessary, please attach an additional page.

Recommender Name (please print): _____

Phone Number _____Campus Email _____

Signature _____ Date _____

Please submit this form by <u>one</u> of the following means by Friday, April 2 at 5:00pm:

- Mail: Kathleen Hanna, University Library, 755 W. Michigan St., Indianapolis, IN 46202
- Fax: (317) 274-7133, Attn. Kathleen Hanna
- Email: file attachment to kgreatba@iupui.edu

Figure 3.2 Example of advertising handout for Diversity Scholar Program

 university library

Undergraduate Diversity Scholar Program

Are you a highly motivated undergraduate interested in increasing diversity and promoting multicultural awareness at University Library and beyond?

Consider applying to be a Scholar and:

- Experience professional level work within a library and university setting
- Gain communication and research skills that can be applied in any career
- Earn $10/hour for 20 hours a week for 10 months, and
- Develop the multicultural awareness of IUPUI students, staff, and faculty.

Autumn Langley
2009–2010 Diversity Scholar   **Application Deadline: Friday, April 2 at 5pm**

For more information and application, visit: www.ulib.iupui.edu/about/diversity/fellowship

among the student population. Applicants for the program noted that they heard about the program from former participants or applicants.

Evaluating the applications

The students were judged on the content and quality of their essays, evidence of previous diversity-related activities, and their Grade Point Average (GPA). Our goal was to attract well-rounded, enthusiastic undergraduates who would thrive in the Program, but we did not want their employment in the library to interfere with their studies or previous commitments. The applications were generally quite strong and it was often difficult to whittle down the list to four or six final candidates.

Figure 3.3	Example of Diversity Scholar applicant evaluation sheet

University Library Diversity Undergraduate Fellowship
2008-2009 Fellowship Selection Committee

Applicant Score Sheet

Applicant Name:_____

> Application requirements:
> 1. Completed fellowship application
> 2. Personal essay on understanding of how to live and work in a diverse society
> 3. Minimum of 2.0 GPA or above
> 4. 2 recommendations

DIRECTIONS FOR SCORING: On a scale of 1 to 5 (1 representing the lowest rate and 5 representing the highest rate), rank the candidate on the following criteria:

CUMULATIVE GPA:

2.0 to 2.4	2.4 to 2.8	2.8 to 3.2	3.2 to 3.6	3.6 to 4.0	
1	2	3	4	5	_____

COMMUNITY INVOLVEMENT: Does the applicant participate in any civic groups, Student organizations, community service, etc.?

| 1 | 2 | 3 | 4 | 5 | _____ |

DIVERSITY AWARENESS AND COMMITMENT: Does the applicant demonstrate an understanding of, and a commitment to diversity?

| 1 | 2 | 3 | 4 | 5 | _____ |

COMMUNICATION SKILLS: Does the applicant adequately express him or herself in the essay? Do the recommendation letters indicate adequate communication skills?

| 1 | 2 | 3 | 4 | 5 | _____ |

TEAM WORK EXPERIENCE: Does the applicant list or discuss experiences that involve team work? Do the recommendation letters indicate the ability to work in a team environment?

| 1 | 2 | 3 | 4 | 5 | _____ |

OVERALL LETTERS OF RECOMMENDATION:

| 1 | 2 | 3 | 4 | 5 | _____ |

COMMENTS:_____

_____   Total Score:_____

_____

The Diversity Council conducted 30-minute face-to-face interviews with the final candidates before selecting two to whom they would offer the positions. Some of our interview questions included:

- How have you used the libraries' resources in your course work?

- Tell us about a time that you worked in a team environment at work, school or volunteering.

- What interested you in applying for this Program?

- What are your career goals?

- What strengths would you bring to this Program?

- Tell us about a time that you've had to take the initiative to get something done.

- If selected for this Program, what do you hope to gain from the experience?

- There can sometimes be tensions when diverse groups/ people come in contact. Tell us how you have dealt with (or would deal with potential) tensions/conflicts.

- One of your recommendation letters describes you as a 'highly motivated'. Can you give us an example of when you've had to use this trait?

The Council also asked about particular experiences or projects that the candidates may have highlighted in their applications, such as starting a student organization or diversity-related work done for a course or in collaboration with a professor.

Hiring and training the Scholars

After the Scholars were selected, the Council devised simple 'ground rules' for organizing the students' time to ensure a smooth transition with staff in the students' work area and with the library's payroll office.

1. You may clock in for work between the hours of 7:30a.m. and 5:30p.m., Monday through Friday.

2. You may be in the UL1115 area for library or school work between the hours of 7:30a.m. and 5:30p.m., Monday through Friday.

3. You may have visitors in the UL1115 area while using the space for school work rather than library work. You are responsible for your visitors' conduct as UL1115 is not a public area.

4. If working more than 8 hours in one day, it is important that you clock out for a lunch or break to ensure that overtime is not accrued.

5. At least 5 hours per week will be devoted to digital library projects. Please clock in under the appropriate digital library account for these 5 hours.

Our new student Scholars met with the library's administration to complete required employment paperwork, including authorizing a background check (required for all employees) and entering their information into the university's online time clock system. The students were e-mailed an orientation schedule for their first week of employment (see Appendix B for sample) to introduce them to the behind-the-scenes environment of the library, meet library staff, finish any personnel paperwork, and settle into their work areas.

Feedback from the Scholars

At the end of their year with us, the Council requested feedback from the Scholars and they offered valuable suggestions for improving the Program. Diversity Scholar Ashley's ideas for enhancement included:

Since there are basically two aspects to the position – creating projects and events for the library and collaborating with different teams in the library on established projects, it would be beneficial if this were a 50–50 split of the duties to ensure a balanced experience.

Have more structure, communication, and teaching. A blueprint to develop the team collaborations is needed and these projects should be in place when the Scholars are hired. Determine what training is needed so the Scholars are brought up to speed quickly and efficiently on the materials and technology they will need to complete the projects.

The unstructured time for the Scholars is extremely valuable as it permits informal brainstorming and research for the self-directed projects, like displays and events.

The feedback process was later formalized by the creation of a brief exit survey:

1. During the course of the program, did you share information you'd learned about research or library resources with your peers? If so, please describe briefly.

2. How did the program change, if at all, your perception of librarianship as a career or academic libraries in general?

3. What aspects of the program do you believe will be most useful to you as you continue your education and/or pursue your desired career path?

4. What did you enjoy most about the program?

5. What aspects of the program could be improved and/or eliminated?

6. What insights, tips would you share with next year's Scholar?

7. Describe the sum of your experience in 5 words (or less).

8. Please share anything else you'd like us to know.

This has helped us to evolve the Undergraduate Diversity Scholar Program by gaining insights such as those shared by some of our other Scholars:

> It really changed my view about librarians. I did not know they work under tenure, and study topics relating to research and information literacy etc. I did not know that librarianship is a science before I got to know and experience the things that librarians do.
>
> I would encourage next year's [scholars] to practice thinking outside the box, and not stick to a specific formula. I think the one drawback of this year's displays is that we didn't really change the format from one display to another. I would have liked to do a display just on some particular concept, such as 'minority' music like jazz, reggae etc. that provide a cathartic outlet for social problems. So I think, given the freedom that we are granted, we should make full use of it and not fall into a groove.
>
> I really learned a lot about the campus environment (what you can and can't do in terms of advertising, which offices are able to help you with certain things, etc.) while planning 'Beyond Stereotypes.' I definitely plan on retaining that knowledge and using it when planning future events with other organizations/campus entities in the future.

Postponed Scholar outreach project to high school students

The Diversity Council discussed the possibility of creating a similar program for high school students, paralleling one begun at Cornell University (Ithaca, NY) (*http://www.library.cornell.edu/diversity/*). It was thought that our Undergraduate Diversity Scholars, having been mentored in our library, could gain additional experience in turn by acting as mentors to local high school students. IUPUI University Library would benefit by extending its outreach beyond the campus and into the community and by fostering the recruitment of minorities to the profession.

Points that were put on the table for discussion to create such a program included:

- High school juniors and seniors would be eligible.
- It would require more structure than our Undergraduate Diversity Scholar Program.
- The objectives of this outreach program would be for the high school students to:
  - be exposed to a university environment and learn college success skills,
  - use the experience as a bridge between high school and college,
  - learn transferable job skills, and
  - gain job experience in a professional environment.
- Possible time frames
  - Fall and/or Spring semester in cooperation with a local high school that followed a similar academic calendar.
  - Summer (our Diversity Scholars are not contracted to work through the summer, but this might be presented as an option).
  - Spring break (dismissed as being an insufficient time period and would conflict with library staff and high school students whose families might have vacation plans).

- Possible work assignments
  - Rotate students through library teams so they would be exposed to the wide range of tasks and aspects of library work. (There would probably be insufficient time to expose the students to all library teams and this may raise training issues and affect the necessary buy-in from the teams.)
  - Students would probably not perform librarian-type assignments but typical hourly employee assignments. (This really does not expose them to the range of work of academic librarians.)
- Develop an incentive to attend IUPUI. For example, if you're a High School Diversity Scholar, the library will guarantee you an hourly job while attending IUPUI, provided you maintain an acceptable grade point average and work performance.

However, after careful consideration, the Diversity Council reached the conclusion that it would be best to strengthen our Undergraduate Diversity Scholar Program over the next few years and table the discussion for a high school outreach program until a later date. As it turned out, this was a wise decision in light of subsequent budget constraints and the issues of Council members' workloads.

Unexpected Scholar issues

Although the University Library Undergraduate Scholar Program encourages students from underrepresented minorities to apply, we had not foreseen problems arising from the application of an undocumented non-US resident student. Although there are undocumented students at IUPUI, they are not permitted by federal law to be employed.

We contacted several other campus units and asked if this issue had arisen with their student employees and the Diversity Council considered reorganizing the program into an academic scholarship rather than an employment situation. We were unable to achieve a solution that would adhere to law and create a level playing field for all Scholar candidates, so unfortunately this issue remains unresolved at this time.

We had also not considered the ramifications of having hourly student workers who enjoyed some freedoms not available to other student workers in the library. Our Diversity Scholars' work spaces are located in a technical support area that is not open to the public; although this area is open during business hours, the Scholars could be granted access to it outside of their normal work hours. Also, the Diversity Scholars were able to set their own work hours, within the limits mentioned above and may even leave the building to perform Scholar-related work elsewhere on campus (e.g. student interviews, meeting with student organizations, etc.). Some library staff were also concerned the Scholars were taking liberties by bringing in visitors and requesting supplies without proper authorization. These issues were discussed with all stakeholders, compromises reached, ruffled feathers smoothed, and more detailed ground rules created for future Scholars (see Appendix B).

An embarrassment of riches

University Library has been extremely fortunate in its Undergraduate Diversity Scholars, who have all proved to be creative, dynamic, and successful students. Each Scholar has put her own stamp (to date all our Scholars have been female) on her projects, many of which are highlighted in the following chapter.

4

Examples of diversity programming and outreach

Abstract: This chapter discusses programs and initiatives developed and executed by the University Library Undergraduate Diversity Scholars to increase awareness of diversity and encourage discussion on campus and in the surrounding community. This chapter also discusses additional ideas for diversity outreach and programming projects and events in academic libraries that IUPUI University Library would either like to expand upon in its current work or pursue in the future.

Key words: diversity, multiculturalism, universities, academic libraries, outreach, campus, community, displays, exhibits, RISE initiative, service, website, blog, Facebook, stereotypes, To Mexico With Love, Hurricane Katrina, Southern University of New Orleans, Southwest Asia, collaboration, grants.

Diversity Scholar campus and community outreach

I have received instruction from Dr Paul Mullins for the past few years and I have taken great interest in his archaeological/anthropological work in the Indianapolis area. I will be proudly presenting an exhibit on the first floor of the library in honor of the African-American community of the Indianapolis area for Black History month. My goal is to raise awareness of the people who inhabited the area that we now so frustratingly park our cars in. Was it a slum neighborhood in need of clearance? Or were there affluent people living here? Did the city paint a picture of a neighborhood in need of removal for the benefit of our university? What repercussions did the community feel, from the IUPUI campus expansion? These are questions I have been exploring in preparation for this project.

Autumn's project for the spring semester tapped into a conflict that had simmered for decades within the African-American community that had been displaced by IUPUI's medical center and university campus.

I have researched several articles and books pertaining to these topics as well as dug up archived photos of Black Student Union protests on campus, oral histories from Charles Hardy, and Joseph Taylor. I hope to be able to provide a nice collection of photos and aerial maps of the area for my exhibit.

To coincide with the exhibit I plan on hosting guest lecturers including Dr Paul Mullins and his research partner Glenn White, and Dr Ian McIntosh from the IUPUI International Affairs office. Dr McIntosh has focused his career on issues of reparations and reconciliation. I envision a lively and beneficial panel discussion with Dr McIntosh and another student, Patricia Jordan, on reparations and privilege. I would like to host some of these events on campus for the purpose of enlightening the student body of the Indianapolis-IUPUI campus area history. I would like to welcome the community to these events to speak openly about their experiences and opinions as well.

Under the direction of her mentor, Dr Paul Mullins, and librarian Jaena Hollingsworth, Autumn contacted campus groups of color and elders from the displaced African-American community. The response was overwhelming and the event resulted in honest, open public discussions representing all viewpoints on the topic. The high attendance from the campus and surrounding community led to positive local media coverage and the promise of further constructive interactions. Funding was solicited and secured by the library from the campus Office of Diversity, Equity and Inclusion to support ongoing primary research on the topic. The library, as part of the special project, created a website (*http://www.ulib.iupui.edu/neighborhood*) at the request of the IUPUI Executive Vice Chancellor and Dean of the Faculties, to introduce students to the story of the neighborhood now occupied by the university. The website features images held by University Library's Special Collections and Archives.

Another event in Spring 2010 allowed the Diversity Council to interact with the campus Gay Lesbian Bisexual Transgender (GLBT) Faculty Staff Council and a community organization, Indiana Transgender Rights Advocacy Alliance (INTRAA). The GLBT Council issued a campus-wide invitation for grant applications to develop projects that 'promote or enhance knowledge, tolerance, sensitivity, and/or develop understanding of GLBT issues and/or the GLBT community through the development of co-curricular academic programming'. The library's Diversity Council submitted a successful grant for $500 that permitted us to purchase DVDs on transgender issues (with public performance rights) and quickly schedule an open viewing of one of the DVDs, followed by a discussion facilitated by a speaker from the INTRAA. The program was well-received and we plan to repeat it in the coming year. We will also track the usage of the new transgender DVDs as a means of measuring the impact of the programming.

Diversity Scholars' library displays and exhibits

Trina and Ashley were the inaugural 2007–2008 IUPUI University Library Undergraduate Diversity Scholars and truly helped define the program for the library and for their successors. The library designated two large floor-to-ceiling display cases on the first floor for Trina and Ashley to create exhibits that highlighted an ethnic history month or other campus outreach event. It is a high traffic area where the library's small café is located. The Scholars used library materials, including books and digitized images from the library's Special Collections and Archives for their displays. The Diversity Council was gratified that the large display cases were made available to Trina and Ashley; we had been promised only two small rolling display cases and were prepared to instruct the Fellows to scale back their plans. Although we'd hoped the Scholars would create monthly exhibits, the larger display cases allowed them to develop more ambitious projects, often with input from student organizations, that could be displayed for longer periods. The displays have turned the first floor lobby into a more welcoming environment that encourages students and visitors to linger over their coffee and snacks.

The 2008–2009 Scholars, Sindhu and Alise, created more ambitious multicultural exhibits that included a computer running looped slideshows of annotated images garnered from one of the library's subscription databases, AccuNet/AP Multimedia Archive, to illustrate day-to-day life, politics, and points of interest in the countries and areas profiled in their displays of Southwest Asia and West Africa. In addition, Sindhu and Alise partnered with the Confucius Institute of IUPUI, Southwest Asian students, and library staff to provide decorative items and clothing for the Southwest Asia display. The display on West Africa coincided with the visit of Ishmael Beah, best-selling author of *A Long Way Gone*, the campus common reader for 2008–2009. The display featured his book about life as a child soldier in Sierra Leone, along with other supporting library materials. Both the Southwest Asia and West Africa displays were extremely popular, in part due to the interviews of Asian and African students and faculty included in the exhibits. Sindhu and Alise talked with the interviewees about differences in educational systems between their home countries and the United States and challenges to adjusting to a new country as well as a new school. Photos of the students and faculty were posted in the display case next to transcripts of the interviews.

Diversity Scholars' online outreach

Sindhu and Alise created online exhibits to accompany their displays, such as for Southwest Asia (*http://www.ulib. iupui.edu/diversityfellows/southwestasia*), which includes suggested readings and films and video interviews with IUPUI students and faculty from Iran, Iraq, Israel, and Saudi Arabia.

Scholars Trina and Ashley used social networking tools to reflect upon their experiences by creating a weblog and launching a Facebook page to market their events, activities, and displays; subsequent Scholars Sindhu and Alise, and 2009–2010 Scholar, Autumn, continued the tradition, each adding her own personal touches. For example, Ashley blogged about her experience recording the oral history of a beloved IUPUI professor, who died shortly thereafter, and Sindhu, a fourth year student from India, commented on the terror attacks in Mumbai in November 2008.

Special programs developed by the Diversity Scholars

In 2009, the Diversity Scholars and Diversity Council presented 'Beyond Stereotypes,' a program based on the 'Living Library' or 'Human Library' (*http://humanlibrary .org/*) concept, originating in Denmark, but adapted to small discussion groups rather than one-on-one conversations. The Scholars developed their own version of the concept, created training materials for the group facilitators they had recruited, (see Appendix C) and designed and distributed marketing materials and t-shirts for the volunteers. The Dean authorized the use of the venue and funds for snacks for the attendees. Extra t-shirts were given to the first several students to enter the event. Facilitators began by introducing themselves and relating brief stories of how they had experienced stereotyping in their lives. People were free to wander from group to group to meet others or simply stay with one discussion group for more in-depth conversations.

'Beyond Stereotypes' was University Library's first major campus outreach programming aimed at increasing understanding and acceptance of people from all different walks of life. Students, faculty and staff were able to come to the library and, instead of looking up books

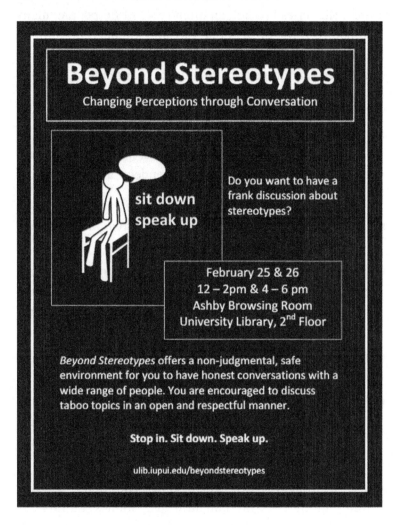

Figure 4.1 Poster and t-shirt design created to advertise 'Beyond Stereotypes' event

or other resources on particular topics related to diversity, talk to actual participants who represented many different backgrounds. The Scholars' main goal with this project was to open up dialogue on campus by addressing what are perhaps taboo topics without regards to 'political correctness'. Held in a quiet, more intimate area of the library, the series boasted an attendance of 66 people, many who had seen the posters that day and attended on impulse between classes. Several professors from a variety of disciplines encouraged their students to attend and follow-up surveys ranked the event highly (see Appendix C).

Comments included: 'It was open, honest,' 'Learned the complications of how much race is an issue,' and '[I enjoyed] hearing others' experiences, we need to talk openly!' Other suggestions by attendees and facilitators for improving the event included:

- Hold the event on one day, rather than two, and schedule it from noon to 2 p.m.

- Find additional ways to market the event besides the campus newsletter and television ads; many students attended on impulse when they saw the posters in the library.

- Additional marketing through the faculty would be beneficial.

- Retain the logo already developed; it is simple and recognizable and we will not have to pay an extra fee for a new t-shirt design when we send the logo to the t-shirt vendor.

- The location was excellent (a quiet, out-of-way reading room in the Payton Philanthropic Studies Library on the second floor of University Library), but the large area rug will need to be moved next time as it impeded wheelchair access for one of our facilitators.

- Facilitators should provide more structure to the conversations and encourage attendees to visit more than one conversation group.

Diversity Scholars and national outreach

I am a Diversity Scholar at IUPUI University Library, as well as an Anthropology student. I have been working on a project with a University Library in New Orleans, to provide them with some resources they are in need of. The University is Southern University at New Orleans. Their library is currently housed in 3 trailers, while they await the rebuilding of their new facility. They lost their entire collection after [Hurricane] Katrina. I have been collaborating with their library director for quite some time now. She has provided me with a list of needs. I am writing you to see if your school might like to contribute to this project by providing some of these needs. We are able to use some of our surplus equipment here at our library for a philanthropic donation to their library.

Our 2009–2010 Diversity Scholar, Autumn, sent the above enquiry to several libraries in the Indianapolis area in the hope of acquiring donations for the library at Southern University of New Orleans (SUNO) (*http://www.suno.edu/About_ SUNO/history.html*), which was devastated by Hurricane Katrina in 2005. At the end of her project in August 2010, 25 computers and a digital projector were shipped to SUNO.

We thought it would be interesting to use this and the account in the following section as examples of how diversity outreach can have an impact beyond the campus and local community.

In 2007, the IUPUI campus began to outline a program to reemphasize its commitment to diversity and learning enrichment programs. In 2009, it launched the RISE Initiative, which focuses on promoting undergraduate research, international learning/study abroad, and service and experiential learning. It is in the spirit of service that Autumn wrote her proposal (see Appendix) to bring resources to another urban university library in need. Her steps in this project included gathering information from the director of the Leonard S. Washington Memorial Library at SUNO as to the library's immediate needs (particularly computer equipment); working with IUPUI University Library's development officer on ideas for fundraising and sources of possible donations; and learning how to use the Foundation Directory Online to research sources for grants and grant writing. Autumn needed to work through several issues inherent in conducting a long-distance project, such as clearing our computer donations through the University's surplus equipment department, identifying sources of funding, and transporting the donations from Indianapolis to New Orleans:

> Matt, Renee and Stacey have been working with me to get the equipment cleared through surplus. [Surplus] needs a donation letter and a copy of SUNO's 501(c)3. I forwarded that info to Ms. Wilson who responded that she has to ask her supervisor about those items. She is not supposed to solicit donations so she is unsure of how to go about the letter. Other than that, Stacey is working on cleaning the hard drives for the computers and Matt is working on a shipping quote. I am mediating between all.

She had also hoped to turn this project into a long-term relationship between the two libraries:

> The Dean [of IUPUI University Library] . . . wants to know where SUNO plans on being in 3–5 years. He

envisions the project that I am creating as a bridge for SUNO. So, I guess what he is wanting is to know what role is our library going to be able to play as far as facilitating SUNO's library long term enhancement?

Autumn acquired a wide range of skills that she was able to carry into her academic work, including collaboration (inside and outside of University Library), proposal development and researching grant sources. She also learned that these processes can often be tedious and, although the project was unable to meet her timeline, it has moved forward and the donations are ready to be transported to their intended destination. The future relationship between IUPUI University Library and Leonard S. Washington Memorial Library at SUNO is as yet undetermined, but the door has been opened to further develop a relationship with another urban university library.

International outreach and the Diversity Scholars

Also in direct response to the campus call to support service, international study, and experiential learning, our 2007–2008 Diversity Scholars, Ashley and Trina, discovered a common interest in a well-established IUPUI summer service learning program held in Cuernavaca, Mexico, called 'To Mexico With Love'. Using a grant award from the Indianapolis Foundation's Library Fund, a modest stipend from University Library, and personal donations from library staff, Ashley and Trina quickly acquired resources for their project to create a library for women and children at La Lagunilla Women's Community Center in Cuernavaca. They assembled and organized a book collection, and traveled to

Figure 4.2 Boys reading in the new library developed by Diversity Scholars Trina and Ashley

Mexico to see their dream come to fruition. Fellow students in the program helped ready the space in the Center as Trina and Ashley developed the new library, created a simple cataloging system, and instructed the adults at the Center in maintaining the library.

The trip to Cuernavaca had a powerful impact on the Diversity Scholars, as demonstrated in one of their weblog postings (*http://diversityfellowship.blogspot.com/*):

> Ashley and I became very, very, very passionate about La Lagunilla and building a library collection for the community. We spent so much time, on and off the clock, working on gathering books, working out ideas, fund raising, and the list goes on. After going to Cuernavaca, Mexico, and meeting and creating relationships with the women and children, we have

more than a passion. We are a part of their community and they are a part of our lives. We will always carry them in our hearts and memories. Ashley and I have discussed the idea of starting a nonprofit so we can continue to stay connected to the colony and develop their library. We have also been discussing annual visits to the colony. It is definite that we want to remain connected to this community.

The Scholars created other online tools to reflect upon their experience: such as a webpage (*http://www.ulib. iupui.edu/about/diversity/fellows#mexico*), and a Microsoft PowerPoint presentation for library staff upon their return from Mexico. Ashley also presented at the Indianapolis Foundation Library Partner's annual meeting. Selected annotated slides also ran on the television monitors used for event advertising in University Library.

Our 2010–2011 Diversity Scholar, Victoria, has pursued another collaboration, described below:

> As a part of the new collaborative teaming with the Office of International Affairs, the University Library Diversity Council will be working on projects aimed at promoting the OIA's 'Partnership Mexico', an initiative working towards the awareness of Mexico's cultures and history through lectures, performances, and other stimulating events. More specifically, the Diversity Council will be working to assist the Office of International Affairs with the promotion of on-campus resources for interested parties, along with visual resources within the University Library to enhance the acknowledgement of Mexican cultures throughout its rich, colorful history, and its influence throughout IUPUI and its surrounding communities. Personally,

I will be working on the promotional displays which will be located in the display cabinets on the first floor of the University Library. In addition to this, I will be aiding in any further ideas that develop to enhance this year-long project. It is an exciting start to my collaborative research with the Diversity Council, and definitely touches upon my long term goals of promoting the ideas of a diverse, collective student body, rather than one divisive of demographics and labels. I am very enthused about this project, and look forward to getting it rolling!

Additional project ideas

The Diversity Council and Scholars have brainstormed ideas for many projects and events in the past three years, but have not yet had time to pursue them all. Some projects rely heavily on collaboration with other campus units and outside sources of funding, but we are also keenly aware of the need to be respectful of others' workloads and time. A few of our other project ideas included:

■ Ask for a representative from IUPUI Adaptive Education Services to host a workshop to train library staff in adaptive technology and classroom skills that will help us work more effectively with our students and patrons with disabilities.

■ We had hoped for a special materials budget to purchase diversity-related materials, but did not receive authorization. Therefore, subject librarians were urged to continue and even increase their efforts to locate titles on diverse topics in their disciplines and apply a portion of their designated materials funds to these purchases. We did not resolve the issue of providing additional resources and materials for the visually-impaired.

■ Conduct an inventory of courses taught at IUPUI that focus on multicultural studies or contain sections on multicultural and diversity issues. This inventory would assist the library in developing programs and collections that support these curricula.

■ The IUPUI Vice Chancellor for Student Life and Dean of Students requested information about the diversity of University Library's collections. Although we have been unable to find an efficient way to inventory our collection, we have suggested that the Diversity Scholars:

- Identify a handful of areas of diversity (e.g. African American Studies, Women's Studies, etc.)
- Research the literature of these disciplines for lists of core, seminal titles.
- Search the library's catalog against this list of titles.

Additional suggestions for outreach and programming

The Diversity Council, Diversity Scholars, and University Library have made great strides on campus, but we are always searching for additional ways to expand our reach to engage more students and increase our value to IUPUI. We have been able to act upon a few of the ideas below; many more await the time and energy which we can devote to them. Many of the suggestions that follow cost only time and commitment.

Outreach

- Contact diverse faculty and staff organizations:

  IUPUI offers numerous opportunities to connect with a wide range of faculty organizations, including the Office for Women, Black Faculty and Staff Council, Latino Faculty Staff Council, LGBT Faculty Staff Council, Native American Faculty Staff Council, Asian American and Pacific Islander Faculty Staff Council. Discussions might range from providing curriculum support by asking for advice on collection development to investigating partnerships for displays and special events.

- Speak to academic advisors:

  Our academic advisors recently formed their own campus professional advising organization, based on the tenets of the National Academic Advising Association (NACADA) (*http://www.nacada.ksu.edu*) and invited IUPUI faculty to attend their first meeting. Academic advisors develop relationships with students from the time they arrive on campus as freshmen and often until they graduate. These are people who should know about the library's commitment to diversity and can help promote the Undergraduate Diversity Scholar Program.

- Arrange formal or informal meetings with diverse student employees:

  These students can be asked to serve on the library's Diversity Council and Student Advisory Group or evaluate targeted initiatives, such as University Library's International Newsroom. They may even serve as 'ambassadors' to promote library initiatives among their peers, particularly if they are active in campus student organizations.

- Arrange to set up information tables at various campus events:

  University Library's Campus Outreach Group, mentioned in the previous chapter, routinely performs outreach at new student orientation, new faculty orientation, and during the first week of fall semester. For example, our 'Weeks of Welcome' table in the library (staffed during the first Tuesday and Wednesday of fall semester) features a homemade tabletop 'wheel of fortune' for students to spin, answer questions about the library and its resources, and prizes (donated by subscription database vendors). This activity always seems to be a hit with our international students. Although often shy about approaching librarians for assistance they are eager to interact with us in this less formal setting. This may give us clues on how to approach them for library instruction.

- Partner with the campus unit that facilitates access for the disabled/special needs students:

  At IUPUI, students who wish to receive special services need to sing up to receive Adaptive Educational Services (AES). University Library has considered hosting workshops by AES (these could be targeted for education majors) or supporting the Movin' On workshop and open house for AES students (*http://diversity.iupui.edu/aes/ movin-on/*).

- Book clubs:

  Work with an existing campus reading group or course to develop a diversity-focused book club. The book clubs could focus on short or long fiction or non-fiction works about diversity issues; shorter works would allow for small, short-term clubs and longer works could be discussed in greater depth. If your campus or community already promotes an annual common reader, this is an excellent place to begin.

■ Work with appropriate residence halls:

University residence halls are often divided into 'theme' houses. For example, at IUPUI we have the Women in Science House and International House. There also exists a program within campus housing, the Mary Cable Social Justice Center, whose values include: 'Promoting understanding between all students that leads to appreciation and celebration of differences' (*http://life .iupui.edu/housing/justice_center.html*).

■ Lend support to student veterans:

IUPUI currently enrolls over 1,500 student veterans returning from recent or current overseas conflicts. University Library currently provides a liaison librarian to the Office for Veterans & Military Personnel (*http:// veterans.iupui.edu/*).

■ Lend support to other academic initiatives for diverse students and faculty:

Librarians at IUPUI have become integrated in programs such as McNair Scholars (for 'low-income, first-generation, and underrepresented students') and Diversity Research Scholars (for minority students) (*http://diversity.iupui .edu/students/opportunities.html*) by providing assistance with grant proposals and instructing students in academic research resources.

■ Join appropriate campus councils and committees:

As faculty, librarians at IUPUI are eligible to serve on numerous campus governing bodies, such as the Faculty Council (*http://www.iupui.edu/~fcouncil/about.html*) and its committees that effect campus policy on inclusion and faculty and student affairs. There is not currently librarian representation on the campus Diversity Cabinet (*http://diversity.iupui.edu/cabinet.html*), so this is an area we can continue to pursue.

■ Embed diversity issues in library instruction:

Simply by tweaking the search examples used in bibliographic and information literacy instruction or in library assignment topics, we can demonstrate librarians' awareness of diversity and multicultural issues. For example:

- Equitable access to education or health care

- Compare and contrast points of view on a current event through different news sources (e.g. *New York Times* vs. *Times of India* vs. a political weblog)

- Research types of music, dance or art students may be unfamiliar with (e.g. find similarities and differences between Hip-Hop music of various ethnicities)

- Compare and contrast political or criminal justice systems from other countries

- Study aspects of women's issues from around the world (e.g. suffrage, abortion, lesbianism, etc.)

- Digital divide.

Also, highlight any diversity-related databases to which the library subscribes, such as Ethnic NewsWatch™ (ProQuest), GenderWatch™ (ProQuest), Opposing Viewpoints in Context™ (Gale), or PAIS International™ (CSA).

Exhibits and digital collections

■ Combine the opening of new displays with low-cost 'launch' events:

For example, when our Diversity Scholars Sindhu and Alise created their display on Southwest Asia, we served inexpensive candies and fruit, typical of those regions.

- Displays for small spaces:

Prominently placed shelves, countertops, niches, and end caps can be used for small, yet effective displays. Use book covers that are normally discarded after cataloging, ALA posters bound into *American Libraries*, or vendor 'freebies' to dress up these displays to make them more eye-catching. We have had several small displays at the reference desk and students often enjoy looking at the books while waiting for assistance.

- Write grants to obtain traveling exhibits from ALA or other sources that support diversity:

The American Library Association is one of many organizations that offers a selection of traveling exhibits (*https://publicprograms.ala.org/orc/travelingexhibitions/ index.html*), many of which are diversity-related and appropriate for academic libraries. (In the past, University Library hosted the ALA's *Frankenstein: Penetrating the Secrets of Nature* for an anniversary celebration.) The National Endowment for the Humanities (NEH) (*http://www.neh.gov*) also offers grant opportunities to acquire exhibits. We would like to challenge ourselves by developing our own traveling exhibits on diversity topics, perhaps by incorporating our digital collections that can be used by local public or school libraries.

- Repository for study abroad projects, multimedia:

Develop an online repository to help document students' study abroad projects, service learning projects, and diversity-related research. This can be especially effective if students have utilized multimedia to capture their experiences.

- Student-created art exhibits:

  We have considered asking IUPUI's Office of International Affairs to coordinate student art exhibits in our International Newsroom. Our new Diversity Scholar Victoria is a photography student and shared a series of portraits in which she portrays people of different ethnicities and genders; it is to become her first exhibit in our library.

- Oral histories in 'student voices':

  With the increasing ease of creating podcasts, the library can rotate short streaming video interviews on its website. The students can respond to a single question ('How does the library meet your needs as a/an [international, minority, non-traditional, etc.] student?') or a brief biography ('Hi, I'm Susan and I'm confined to a wheel-chair. This is what a typical day on campus is like for me').

Events

- Book fairs:

  University Library has often partnered with local, inner-city schools to run a Scholastic Book Fair (*http://www.scholastic.com/bookfairs*) to raise money for school libraries to improve and increase their collections and materials. University Library staff, SLIS students, and others volunteer to run the book fair. Primary customers are IUPUI staff, faculty, and students who may purchase books for themselves or the partner school. A portion of the proceeds goes to the school and staff can purchase books from Scholastic on their own.

- Targeted orientation for international students:

  We've learned in the course of research for this book that academic libraries around the world have a great deal in common, but also many differences. International students' expectations of the campus library may be poles apart. An orientation or open house before the start of the fall semester, perhaps as informal as a 'Weeks of Welcome' table (see above), will help the students feel more comfortable with the library staff and vice versa. This would also be an excellent way to find out what workshops, if any, they feel would be most beneficial to them in their course work and academic careers.

- Multicultural juvenile collection:

  The IUPUI School of Library and Information Science is located in the University Library and, in support of that program, our library has a juvenile collection of over 7,500 fiction, non-fiction, and reference titles. This offers opportunities for several possible events, such as:

  □ A 'story hour' event or students' story exchange. Groups of diverse students can read or talk about books their parents read to them or that they enjoyed reading as they were growing up. Are there books or stories we all know? Are there similar stories with variations from across cultures? Are these stories all written or are some in oral traditions?

  □ Display of children's books that teach tolerance and diversity (e.g. *Ten Things I Hate About Me* by Randa Abdel-Fattah, *One World, One Day* by Barbara Kerley, *Daddy, Papa, and Me* by Leslea Newman, etc.).

An event or display focusing on children's literature also offers opportunities for a partnership with local elementary or secondary schools. For example, IUPUI's Center for Young Children (for ages two through kindergarten) often collaborates with other campus units.

- Hip-Hop Night at the Library:

  Using the research into Hip-Hop music of various ethnicities (see above), host a music and dance night in the library before the start of the semester or as a way to reduce stress during finals week. Use appropriate CDs from the library's collections or ask students to bring their own. See if another campus unit, such as a music school, or a local business is willing to loan the electronic equipment. If there is insufficient space in the library for the event, hold it outdoors (weather permitting), or in the student center or union.

- Poetry slam:

  IUPUI promotes a poetry contest among local high school students, most of whom are from African-American, Hispanic, and low-income households. The library can partner with the poetry contest coordinator to host a poetry slam on campus that would not only allow students to perform their poetry for the community, but perhaps introduce them to the IUPUI campus.

- Support of different ethnic celebration months with speakers or panels:

  Many universities across the United States have special events for multicultural celebration months. The library can support campus efforts by providing venues for speakers, creating exhibits, and highlighting the diversity of its collection.

- Flash mob:

  Promote diversity and campus-wide discussion by scheduling flash mobs, which are growing in popularity worldwide. This would be an extremely effective means of celebrating diversity or to launch a library or campus event. This may also offer possibilities for collaboration with student or community actors or performance artists. At IUPUI, it could be facilitated by our campus interactive theater troupe, A.C.T-Out Ensemble, which focuses on social issues.

- Video flash mob:

  Invite interested student groups to create short videos on what they do in the library, how they use the resources, etc., and post to the library's website and permit them to use the videos for recruitment and publicity for their own organizations.

- Mid-term exams and final exams week game nights:

  At this writing, IUPUI University Library is developing a 'game night' to promote study breaks and tension-relieving socializing during the most stressful times during the academic year. The original plan was to provide popular board games and other materials, but we decided to feature a variety of games from around the world, such as Mancala (Africa).

- 'Old' meets 'new':

  Develop an event at which traditional students may meet and talk about their different perspectives on college life with non-traditional students. Possible discussions between them might include:

  - Why did you return to school or what delayed your enrollment until now?

  - If you previously attended college, what differences do you see today?

- How do you approach your classes? Your study habits?

- How do you balance your studies with your job, family, and other responsibilities?

- Are you the first in your family to receive a university education?

Special collaborations

■ Invite a disability expert to evaluate the library space for accessibility:

This evaluation may include not only how the disabled are able to navigate the library's physical space (stairs, elevators, restrooms, comfort in accessing service points), but may also result in suggestions for technology improvements, better signage, and ways that staff engage those with diverse abilities. The key is to consider all suggestions and make changes based on the expert's recommendations.

■ Partner with other campus unit diversity committees:

Our campus unit diversity committees (*http://diversity .iupui.edu/planning/*) offer opportunities for collaboration and resource sharing. This is especially effective if you can locate sources for funding or grants.

■ Locate community partners:

Indianapolis has a number of museums and cultural centers that have a history of reaching out to academic partners through deferred admission fees (Eiteljorg Museum of American Indians and Western Art) and exhibits (Indiana State Museum). Indianapolis is also home to a Mexican Consulate that may be interested in developing relationships to help the library work with

Hispanic students, for example. In addition, over 100 different languages are spoken in the state of Indiana and many ethnic communities have social and professional organizations.

5

Building bridges: developing the International Newsroom

Abstract: This chapter discusses the planning and development of the International Newsroom at IUPUI University Library, how the project has evolved since its launch, and offers advice to other libraries that would like to develop similar projects.

Key words: diversity, multiculturalism, universities, academic libraries, outreach, international television, international news.

Indiana University's call for diversity initiatives

In keeping with the great work done by the Diversity Scholars and their supervisors in creating programs and displays and developing partnerships with libraries and communities both in the United States and internationally, the Diversity Council was searching for additional opportunities to provide IUPUI students with an initiative that would increase awareness of diversity issues. In September 2008, Indiana University President Michael McRobbie announced the President's University Diversity Initiative, a $1million program to 'fund meritorious proposals that support the continued enhancements in the development of the racial, ethnic, and cultural diversity of all IU campuses as well as to enrich the equity of access for IU students from underrepresented communities' [*http:// diversity.iupui.edu/univ_initiative.html*]. This initiative was designed to provide $100,000 over three years to selected projects.

University Library's Diversity Council decided to submit a proposal for an International Newsroom, which would provide international television news broadcasts for our students, and also provide newspapers and magazines from representative countries. One of our Council members had read about a similar project developed in the James Branch Cabell Library at Virginia Commonwealth University (VCU). [It should be noted that as of March 9, 2009, this newsroom was closed due to declining use and budgetary issues. Diversity Scholars Alise and Sindhu suggested that the broadcasts be provided in foreign languages to give our international students 'news from home' in their native languages.

University Library's proposal

The greatest challenge we faced in planning the International Newsroom was the short deadline given for submitting proposals (which seems to be an all too common issue at universities). Although the Initiative was announced in mid-September, the deadline for 'pre-proposals' was October 7, 2008. This meant we needed to do our research quickly and work as team to flesh out our plan. The Council took the advice of our Diversity Scholars to offer news in the languages of our international students, which necessitated looking closely at student enrollment data provided by IUPUI's Admissions Office. We learned IUPUI has large populations of students from China, India, Saudi Arabia,

Taiwan, Canada, Iran, Mexico, Nigeria and Japan. We also have large numbers of African American, Asian/Pacific Islander, and Hispanic/Latino students, and a few Native American students. Additionally, we wished to provide our international students with copies of newspapers in their native languages. We decided that the languages we would focus on would be Arabic, Japanese, Chinese, Spanish, Hindi and at least one African dialect.

Although the pre-proposal was a bit sketchy, the Diversity Council was invited to tender a full proposal, which needed to be submitted within two weeks. Since we had already decided upon the types of resources we wished to provide and in which languages, the next step was to quickly determine the availability and cost of such resources. Diversity Scholar Sindhu was very knowledgeable about various television outlets for international news and provided a number of possibilities for consideration. Council member Jennifer researched the availability and pricing of international newspapers using our subscription database, *Ulrich's International Periodical Directory*. University Library had gradually discontinued international newspaper subscriptions over several years, mostly due to the expense and delay in receiving overseas delivery; we thought this an excellent time to see if there had been improvements in delivery mechanisms and if there would be renewed interest among our growing international student population. With news outlets in mind, we set about finding the best provider.

There were several factors to consider when selecting a provider, including cost, hardware, contracts, and programming. During our research, we located SCOLA, a non-profit organization that 'retransmits educational television programming from around the world via satellite, cable, and the Internet' (*http://www.scola.org*). We quickly contacted SCOLA to obtain a price quote to include in our proposal; the necessary hardware and access would be costly but they did provide programming for the languages and regions in which we were interested.

We consulted our in-house technical support team for help selecting and pricing flat screen televisions and computer workstations that would be available to users to access a portal to a variety of online news sources that we would pay a webmaster to set up and maintain. Additionally, we worked with the library's administration office to find appropriate vendor catalogs to price comfortable furniture for the space.

One important detail was to determine where in the library the International Newsroom would be located. Our microforms collection, very much underused and outdated, took up a large portion of the high-traffic second floor reference area. The Dean of the Library approved the potential move of the microforms collection out of this 'prime real estate' and into an area that was still accessible to both library staff and patrons. This also gave librarians an impetus to weed the microforms collection, as the new microforms area would not accommodate the existing collection in its entirety. The expense of weeding and moving was included in the Council's proposal.

Admittedly, we had underestimated the costs of newspaper subscriptions and satellite or cable television service in our preliminary proposal, so we sought to correct this in the final proposal. Once the pricing for the relocation of the microform collection, the computers and televisions, the furniture, the necessary hardware for the satellite connection, and the annual subscriptions to newspapers and satellite feeds was determined, the full proposal was submitted just prior to the deadline. The Council's full proposal may be found in Appendix D.

A second chance at the project

On November 3, 2008, the Council received an e-mail that stated 'although your project shows potential, it was not recommended to the chancellor to be submitted to the Indiana University Office of Equity, Diversity, and Multicultural Affairs for the President's University Diversity Initiative'. The response was disappointing, but fortunately all our hard work was not in vain. The Dean continued to support the project and gave it over to the library's Director of Development to continue searching for possible funding sources, including corporate sponsorship (the microforms area was originally sponsored by National City Bank when the current library was constructed in 1992). While the Diversity Council would no longer have direct responsibility for the International Newsroom, our initial planning and vision would help shape its development. In March 2009, we received word that the library was awarded a grant through the Library Services and Technology Act (LSTA) (*http://www.lsta.org/*) for $8,000 to be used to purchase six flat screen televisions. Additionally, we received a $20,000 grant from the IUPUI Learning Environments Committee for furniture that would be selected by the University Architect's Office. The LSTA grant is a federal 'pass-through grant', meaning the funds were given to the Indiana State Library and then distributed to IUPUI University Library.

Since these two new grants were substantially less than the budget for our original proposal to the University Diversity Initiative, we needed to adjust and prioritize our plan for the International Newsroom and proceed in phases. The initial phase would include seating and televisions with international news programming. The newspapers, computers and portal that we envisioned would have to be put on hold until additional sources of funding could be located. We also began to question the wisdom of including print newspapers and other publications in this area. Our sense is that fewer and fewer people, particularly technology-savvy students, read print publications, instead preferring to acquire current news instantly by television or through Internet sources.

While SCOLA provided attractive programming, the costs of hardware and broadcast access were prohibitively high. Our in-house technical support team researched other possible sources for our needed programming and decided that Dish® Network would be the most practical for our needs. While the pricing was similar to other providers, Dish® was found to have a better selection of international news channels for the areas that we wanted, although they did not provide coverage from Africa. We eventually selected news packages that included the Middle East, India, China, Korea, Europe and Latin America in their native languages. Our European selection, EuroNews, provided coverage in English.

Construction and furnishing of the International Newsroom

From March through September 2009, many people worked on making the International Newsroom a reality. First, the space needed to be cleared. The microform collection needed to be weeded and moved to a new location. Extra cabinets needed to be sent to surplus or donated to other area libraries. This author is proud to note that no microfilm or fiche found its way into local landfills. It was all donated to various schools and organizations to be used in art projects. Once the area was clear and cleaned, televisions had to be mounted to the walls, furniture selected, ordered and delivered, and wiring needed to be installed and a mechanism for listening to the news determined.

In initial planning, Dean Lewis advised the Council that he preferred the International Newsroom would have a welcoming, relaxing atmosphere, but would not be a 'clubhouse' that would disrupt activities at the reference

Figure 5.1 Microform area designated for conversion to International Newsroom

desk, only a few yards away. To prevent this, our technical support team wired the televisions so that the audio would play on transmitters attached to large immovable tables in the International Newsroom. Students could plug in their headphones or tune into the frequencies on their own FM radios or those that we had available at the circulation desk to promote the project. The library sells the small radios with ear buds for $2.50, having obtained them on clearance for a few pennies less per radio. Signage indicated to students which television was connected to which transmitter or which frequency was required for radio reception.

Figure 5.2   International Newsroom in process

Figure 5.3 International Newsroom in process

Figure 5.4 Current configuration of International Newsroom

Changes to the International Newsroom

The International Newsroom opened to the public on September 1, 2009, taking less than a year to realize, but our greatest challenges lay ahead. Although we publicized the Newsroom through various venues, including student orientation activities inside and outside the library, we observed very few students watching the programming in the International Newsroom, even after several weeks of classes.

We did know of one avid fan, a student who rather apologetically informed Mindy Cooper that our news feed from India was *not* broadcast in Hindi (as we had advertised) but another dialect entirely. Mindy thanked him, and with assistance from our technical support expeditiously located an alternate news broadcast and verified that it indeed was in Hindi.

Faculty members had not brought their classes into the area and the School of Journalism was disinterested in our end product. By December 2009, the Council was discussing making changes. We realized that in our quest to be inclusive of our international students, we may actually have been too *ex*clusive of our other patrons. Having news coverage in Hindi, Arabic, Spanish, Korean and Mandarin appeared to have a negative effect on the number of people who would actually be able to understand the access we were providing. One major setback, according to a faculty member from the IU School of Journalism, was the lack of closed captioning in English for those who did not speak the language. We looked into this issue and determined that closed captioning, a requirement by the US Federal Communications Commission, was not universal and the few channels that provided captioning provided it in the native language, not

| Table 5.1 | | Original program channels and updated English language channels |

Region/Language	Native Language Channel	English Language Channel
Middle East	Al Jazeera	LinkTV
India	Telegu	Headlines Today
China	CCTV-4	CCTV-9
Korea	WOW-TV	KBS World
Europe	EuroNews	EuroNews
Spanish	CNN en Español	CNN en Español

English. So by February 2010, we had found alternative channels to provide news from the Middle East, India, China and Korea and in English. Only EuroNews and CNN en Español were retained from the original programming lineup.

With this change in programming, we also had to expand our definition of 'news'. While the channels we had originally selected were entirely centered on serious news broadcasts, some of the new channels provided popular culture programs interspersed throughout their daily broadcast, which we hoped would actually attract more of our students as they pursue study abroad and other opportunities at IUPUI.

We recently provided access to coverage of the 2010 FIFA World Cup, but had disappointing attendance, due to factors beyond our control: maintenance in other areas of the library that resulted in construction noise and loss of air conditioning systems, plus competition from our IUPUI Campus Center which also broadcast the World Cup events. Students may also have felt uncomfortable expressing unrestrained enthusiasm for the games and feared being 'shushed' by overzealous library staff. We still hope to provide some special programming and events that will draw viewers to the space outside their normal activities and that we can eventually foster some sense of community through the Newsroom.

Future of the International Newsroom

As the recent changes illustrate, the International Newsroom is continually evolving. We will make adjustments to the programming as necessary, either as channels are added or dropped from packages, or by patron feedback. Assessment will be a very important ongoing part of our project. We have begun plans for evaluating student use of the International Newsroom by employing existing library security cameras in that area to unobtrusively observe patron use of the space and determine whether our efforts to alter programming, reconfigure seating, and improve marketing efforts result in increased patronage. We are planning surveys that we hope will shed light on our students' opinions of the space and their ideas for programming and future special events (see Chapter 7). We believe that student surveys and the use of the area by faculty and their classes will help the Diversity Council develop an International Newsroom that will provide needed and wanted coverage of news and events to the entire IUPUI community.

6

Sharing the wealth: other library departments and diversity initiatives

Abstract: This chapter discusses projects developed by staff other than University Library's Diversity Council and Undergraduate Diversity Scholars. These are endeavors that librarians in a wide variety of academic libraries, including those with small staffs that will not sustain a separate diversity council or committee, may adjust to fit their own needs and circumstances. The chapter concludes with important questions to consider when planning diversity projects.

Key words: diversity, multiculturalism, universities, academic libraries, outreach, American Library Association, READ campaign, digital collections, Archive of Muslim American History and Life, Bulletin of the Santayana Society, Flanner House, Ransom Place, Saoirse – Irish Freedom, oral histories.

Increasing involvement throughout the library

While the Diversity Council and the Scholars work hard to provide outreach and programming to the IUPUI community and beyond, other teams and committees, as well as individual librarians, have also contributed to the efforts to increase diversity awareness.

One ongoing project was launched in the Diversity Council by members who decided to create READ posters to display around the library and in various campus locations and was later adopted on a wider scale by the Campus Outreach Group (COG). READ posters, marketing tools developed and made available by the American Library Association (ALA) READ campaign (*http://www .alastore.ala.org/readdesignstudioinfo/default.aspx*), consist of images of people against a customized background, holding their favorite books as a means to promote the importance of reading and literacy. ALA's stock posters for purchase feature famous people and celebrities – actors, musicians, authors, and athletes, for example, who appeal to a diverse audience of children and adults. During a Council meeting, Diversity Scholar Trina suggested the READ posters as a way for the library make a connection with the campus. She had seen READ posters in school libraries while growing up and felt that our subject librarians and library staff could be our campus 'celebrities'.

The ALA makes various software packages available for libraries to purchase and create their own READ posters. University Library was granted funding to purchase the software and we also obtained a photo quality printer which enabled us to print our 13' × 9' posters in-house, rather than having to contract this out to the campus printing services, which resulted in considerable savings.

The project required some initial training on the ALA software and Microsoft Photoshop. Our READ posters feature subject librarians and library staff whose images not only educate the IUPUI community about their subject librarians, but also highlight the diversity of University

Library's staff. The librarians and staff members chose their own books to hold for their photography session and their choices reveal as much about their interests and personalities as they do about their duties in the library. As Diversity Scholar Trina wrote in her blog:

> I think it was a fabulous idea to help create a more friendly environment ... and an environment that shows our diversity but also shows our patrons and employees who WE are ... as an institution. As librarians. As people. Now, our library can be more familiar ... by putting our pictures on these READ posters people will look at us, our names and positions. I am very confident that by showing our faces, it makes us more approachable. The patrons will feel like they know us. But this project has a deeper significance. I wanted to tear down the invisible wall of discrimination between part-timers, full-timers, and *student* workers. This is a project that brings all of us together, to participate in some fun. This project shows that we are all important.

While members of the Diversity Council worked on the initial set of posters, the project was eventually given to the library's Campus Outreach Group (COG), a small group of librarians who spearhead the marketing of the library's services and resources. This move freed the Diversity Scholars and Council members to work on other projects. Creating READ posters is an ongoing project and, as posters are completed, they are hung in public areas in the library and often additional copies are shared with librarians' liaison schools or departments for display. The Diversity Council and COG have also posted a gallery of our READ posters on University Library's Flickr® account (*http://www.flickr.com/photos/19385826@N06/sets/72157622253141959/*) and posters also appear on JagTV, the campus closed-circuit television system.

Figure 6.1   Robin Crumrin's READ poster

Figure 6.2   2010–2011 Diversity Scholar Victoria's READ poster

Using diverse digital collections to create community partnerships

While COG has the READ posters, other library teams have developed their own projects to highlight diversity. University Library's Digital Libraries Team, led by Robin Crumrin, partnered with the Crispus Attucks Museum and its Board of Advisors to create the Crispus Attucks Museum digital collection. Crispus Attucks Museum is located only a few blocks from the IUPUI campus in an historically African American school. This was one area of the local community that was not displaced by the IUPUI and medical center construction and expansion described in Chapter Four.

The collection of digitized yearbooks and student newspapers continues to grow and is described on the library's website (*http://www.ulib.iupui.edu/digitalscholarship/ collections/CAttucks*):

> Crispus Attucks was Indianapolis' first segregated high school built for African-Americans in 1927. It was named after Crispus Attucks, a black man who was the first American to die in the Boston Massacre in 1770, a precursor to the American Revolutionary War. In 1986, the school converted from a high school to junior high school. This digital collection captures the history of the high school through its yearbooks (1928–1986), newspapers, and graduation programs.

This digitized collection also entreats those with Attucks yearbooks, graduation programs, and student newspapers to contact the library to fill in missing artifacts from 1930, 1937, and 1980, thereby soliciting additional community input to complete the series. Creating this digital collection and offering open access to it serves scholars from IUPUI, central Indiana, and around the world, but also brings pride to those community members and their relatives included in the yearbooks and graduation programs featured in the collection. This successful partnership with Crispus Attucks, funded with grant monies by the Indianapolis Foundation's Library Fund, will no doubt pave the way for further similar collaborations in our community.

University Library has long sought out partnerships and funding to support digitization projects that further diversity, even prior to the campus mandate, including:

- Archive of Muslim American History and Life (*http://www .ulib.iupui.edu/digitalscholarship/collections/AMAHL*) – In collaboration with the IU School of Liberal Arts at IUPUI, this digital archive collects and preserves documents related to Muslim American history from the colonial era to the present. It includes memoirs, newspapers, books, reports, speeches and other documents that reveal the place of Muslims in American social, political, religious, cultural, and economic life.

- Bulletin of the Santayana Society (*http://www.ulib .iupui.edu/digitalscholarship/collections/Santayana*) – The Santayana Society is an international and interdisciplinary organization, founded in 1980, to further work on The Santayana Edition specifically and to promote Santayana scholarship generally. George Santayana was a Spanish born philosopher, poet, critic, and novelist.

- Flanner House (Indianapolis, Ind.) Records, 1936–1992 (*http://www.ulib.iupui.edu/special/collections/philanthropy/ mss004?show=images*) – Flanner House has provided social services to African Americans in Indianapolis since its establishment as a settlement house for a migrant, rural population arriving from the South at the end of the nineteenth century.

- Ransom Place (*http://www.ulib.iupui.edu/digitalscholarship/ collections/RansomPlace*) – This collection consists of various pieces of material culture collected from anthropology professor Paul Mullins and his Archaeology Field School participants. The items have been recovered from various locations in and around the IUPUI campus, and depict an active and vibrant African American community that once inhabited the area. The IUPUI Archaeology Field School has been conducting excavations in the Ransom Place and Indiana Avenue area since 1999. Material culture from the excavations along with oral historical research is used to interpret African-American culture, class, consumption, race and racism in Indianapolis.

- Saoirse – Irish Freedom (*http://www.ulib.iupui.edu/ digitalscholarship/collections/IrishNews*) and Sovereign Nation (*http://www.ulib.iupui.edu/digitalscholarship/ collections/SNation*) – *Saoirse – Irish Freedom* is the monthly newspaper of the Irish political party Republican Sinn Fein. The name is taken from '*Irish Freedom – Saoirse*', which was a Fenian paper of the early 1910s. IUPUI University Library has collaborated with the School of Liberal Arts to digitize and chronologically display older issues of the newspaper which were previously unavailable online. *The Sovereign Nation* is the on-line and hard copy newspaper of the 32 County Sovereignty Movement founded on December 7, 1997. 'The founders considered themselves a "Committee" of Provisional Sinn Fein, but after being expelled from that organization they formally organized themselves as the 32 County Sovereignty Movement.'

Special Collections and Archives: oral histories

While the Crispus Attucks collection contains actual physical artifacts, work has been initiated to create an oral record of important places and people at and around IUPUI. Diversity Scholar Ashley worked with University Library's

Special Collections Team to record an oral history of Angenieta Biegel, a prominent professor at the Indiana University School of Medicine. Unfortunately, Dr Biegel passed away before the project was completed. And as there was no signed waiver, the material collected cannot be shared. But the experience had a profound impact on Ashley, as evidenced in her blog,

> Dr Biegel was Professor Emerita at the IUMC and was a member of the IUPUI family. She was one of the first women to receive many great medical distinctions and honors through the university. Sadly Dr Biegel passed away April 11, 2008. I only had the opportunity to meet with her three times, but my life was truly enriched with her presence. She was kind, extremely hospitable, and feisty. She also had a wealth of information and knowledge and I only wished I had the opportunity to get to know her better.

Another oral history project that will have a profound effect on not only those conducting the research, but an entire community, is the work being done by an Anthropology class in collaboration with the IUPUI School of Liberal Arts. The library's liaison to the Department of Anthropology and our Digital Scholarship Librarian are assisting Anthropology students in gathering oral histories of those residents living in an historically and predominantly Jewish neighborhood, which is now home to a more broadly diverse population. The Indianapolis Neighborhood Resource Center project is just getting underway, but IUPUI librarians are playing an integral part in helping students collect and preserve data that highlights the diversity of people and places in and around IUPUI that will be available for generations to come.

Tips and suggestions

There is no limit to the number of projects that can be done, not only by a Diversity Council, but by other individuals and departments throughout the library and there are few creative ideas that cannot be scaled down or modified due to staffing, funding, or other constraints.

Some important factors to consider in the planning stages:

- In what diversity issues or projects have your library staff expressed a passion or interest?

- Which projects are most feasible to pursue based on the current campus diversity climate?

- Does the project support the library and campus mission and vision statements?

- What partnerships or collaborations can be established in the library, on campus, or in the local community?

- Which projects are most feasible to pursue based on available resources, including time, money, and space? Some questions to bear in mind:

  - How would the project impact the workload of all collaborators and stakeholders?

  - Is any necessary technology currently in place or would it need to be purchased? Or does another collaborator in the project have the needed technology and is willing to share?

  - Is there a stakeholder in the project who can offer funding or will grant funding if needed? Is there sufficient time to research, write, and submit a grant proposal?

- If the project is deemed important but sufficient resources are unavailable, can the project be done on a more modest scale or developed in stages or increments?

- How will you assess the success, use, or results of your diversity events, final products, or projects?

The following chapter will tackle the sticky issue of assessment of diversity initiatives at IUPUI University Library.

7

Assessing programming and outreach

Abstract: This chapter discusses the importance of assessment in programming and outreach and methods in which the diversity of University Library's staff and collections and the success of its diversity initiatives have been or will be measured.

Key words: diversity, multiculturalism, universities, academic libraries, assessment, surveys, qualitative assessment.

Importance of assessment

Unfortunately, many academic librarians have little background in formal assessment methods (or instruction or event planning, for that matter) and as is the case in most enthusiastic endeavors, assessment is generally an afterthought rather than a part of the planning process. We at IUPUI University Library are no exception and we find ourselves in the uncomfortable position of 'playing catch-up' in this area, particularly as budgets continue to tighten and some may believe that diversity initiatives in the library constitute a luxury rather than a necessity.

'Constructing and implementing diversity initiatives involves continuous experimentation, assessment, modification and innovation. Assessment of diversity is an ongoing lifetime process of improvement', states Love (2001). As institutions of higher education attract more and more diverse students and faculty who may benefit from library diversity initiatives and as budgets tighten, necessitating accountability for time and money, assessment has become more important than ever.

Librarians must determine what needs to be assessed and how to go about it. In terms of diversity, the library's collections, resources, and staff can and should be assessed on an ongoing basis. Initiatives and programs, including those aimed at library staff, as done by Texas A&M University (Yang and White, 2007), and those focused on students, staff and faculty at a university such as IUPUI should also be assessed to determine the effectiveness of promoting and reflecting diversity.

Assessing the diversity of the library collection

But just because assessment should be done, does not mean that it is always easily done. One of the goals identified by our Diversity Council in 2009 was to evaluate the diversity of our collections. Several members of the Council performed literature searches to identify best practices for such an evaluation, as conventional collection evaluation techniques were deemed unsuitable or too labor intensive, but they located very little on the subject at the time. And as work on the International Newsroom and other projects took center stage, the task of evaluating the collection was set aside. In the interim, some practical options for conducting a collection assessment have become known to us.

One possible method, which might still be a tedious task even with our electronic library systems, would be to compare lists of monograph titles purchased prior to the library's Diversity Council activities to a list of those purchased after librarians had been exposed to these initiatives and become more aware of the University Library's goals for increasing diversity. We have also recently become aware of an online resource, *Guide to Reference* (*http://www.guidetoreference.org*), which is 'a selective guide to the best reference sources, organized by academic discipline and published by the American Library Association' that seeks to identify core reference titles in a wide variety of disciplines. The lists available here could serve as an excellent guide to inventorying our own collection to determine if the library owns the best possible sources focused on diversity issues and diverse groups of people. Given the continuing focus on diversity, no doubt other such tools will be developed and best practices will begin to appear in the literature. But in the meantime, it is also useful to invite faculty members, particularly those from diverse groups, to discuss their opinions about the diversity of the library's collection, how they use it, if it fulfills their own research needs, and how best to improve weak areas. They will no doubt be invaluable in identifying seminal or recent works in many areas.

Evaluating use of the International Newsroom by observation and student surveys

While work needs to be done on evaluating our collection, we are planning a few different methods to assess the effectiveness of the International Newsroom (see Chapter 5). Before the Newsroom was installed, digital cameras were strategically placed around the room as part of another assessment project. These cameras permit unobtrusive observation of how many people occupy the space and how they use it and had, in fact, been used by a SLIS faculty member to study the use of the library's Academic Commons computer clusters a few years ago. Although the Newsroom opened in August 2009, we have retained camera footage only since December 2009 and now need to develop a strategy to effectively evaluate the information we are gathering.

Initially, students appeared to use the space simply as another study area, but since the large library tables were removed from the space and replaced with more casual chairs and seating for the fall 2010 semester, there appear to be more students viewing the television screens, even while they seem to be working on their laptop computers. We plan to use samples of earlier security camera footage as a baseline and compare it to samples of this semester's footage to determine the impact, if any, that the change in seating has had on the use of the Newsroom. We will be able to identify peak use times, which televisions the students gravitate to, and if they appear to be performing other tasks while watching the broadcasts, if they ignore the televisions altogether, or if they are only watching the programs.

Another assessment method came about very quickly and serendipitously, proving once again the necessity of being an agile group that can respond to opportune moments. We had been under the impression that no class had visited and used the International Newsroom as part of their course work. As it happened, one instructor had brought a class in during fall 2009 semester without contacting library staff and somehow without attracting much attention. In fall 2010, she spoke with a librarian she had approached to work with her introductory

Figure 7.1   Class visit to International Newsroom

International Studies course. The librarian consulted
Mindy Cooper about recent changes to the International
Newsroom and options for a class of 25 students to
view and listen to the broadcasts. We had recently removed
the large library tables, which had been the anchors
for the headphone plug-in jacks in front of each television,
and had not yet reinstalled the jacks in smaller tables.
Therefore, we had turned up the volume slightly on the
televisions, making it possible for those in close proximity
to listen without headphones or dial into a specified FM
frequency on small radios. For this class, each student was
supplied with a radio to use during class and told they
could keep it to use in the Newsroom in the future. After
the class, each student was given a survey to complete on a
half sheet of paper and asked to respond to questions
about which televisions they had watched, the helpfulness
of the programming in completing their assignment, and
their overall impressions of the International Newsroom.
(See Appendix E).

Figure 7.2 Example of student survey

International Newsroom INTL I100–Study Survey

1. Which television/stations(s) did you watch? Please check all that apply:
   ☐ TV1 - LinkTV
   ☐ TV2 - Headlines Today (India)
   ☐ TV3 - CCTV-9 (China)
   ☐ TV4 - KBS World (Korea)
   ☐ TV5 - EuroNews (Europe)
   ☐ TV6 - CNN en Español

2. What did you watch?
   ☐ News
   ☐ Sports
   ☐ Popular programming
   ☐ Other (please specify) _____

3. How helpful was the programming in completing your assignment?

	Not very helpful	Somewhat helpful	Very helpful	Not applicable
TV1				
TV2				
TV3				
TV4				
TV5				
TV6				

4. This area is a comfortable place to view international news.

Strongly disagree	Somewhat disagree	Neutral	Somewhat agree	Strongly agree
☐	☐	☐	☐	☐

5. Comments?

Results of the International Newsroom survey

Although the 22 student responses we received from the survey hardly constitute a large sample, they will prove useful to begin a focused evaluation of the television programming and furniture configuration. We plan to improve the survey and include a question about the listening method used by each student to determine which option is preferred. It is also possible to create this as an online survey that the faculty member or librarian can load into the university's course management system and permit the student to complete the survey in the context of the class. This would also allow the faculty member to receive the feedback and attach completion of the survey to points or a grade. The results of this class survey included:

- The least watched broadcast was TV2 – Headlines Today (India). The difference in the number of students who watched TV2 compared to the other channels was not significant; this leads us to believe that most of the students wandered about the room and at least glanced at all the televisions during their class period.

- While over 95 percent of the students watched news programming, more than half also watched sports and/or popular programming. Comments from some of the students indicated they also viewed a documentary program and a 'soap opera'. TV4 – KBS World (Korea) broadcasts soap operas at the hour of the morning the class was in the Newsroom. One student commented 'love TV4!' so it seems the idea of popular programming is appealing to students and may prove to be an excellent means of learning about other cultures.

- The majority indicated that TV3 – CCTV-9 (China) and TV5 – EuroNews (Europe) were most helpful in completing their assignment.

- Over 85 percent of the class found the Newsroom to be a very comfortable space.

Obtaining faculty feedback about the International Newsroom

While the surveys have been an unexpected and significant starting point, feedback from the International Studies instructor, Dr Dawn Whitehead, who is also Director of International Curriculum, has been absolutely invaluable. We asked her a series of questions about how she used the International Newsroom and its resources in developing the assignment for her course. We also asked her thoughts on the changes we had made in the physical space. She kindly allowed us to relate her responses verbatim below.

What do you think about the removal of the study tables and the addition of the soft seating and café tables?
I think this was a great modification. It makes the area more relaxed and user friendly. I would also stay longer with the more comfortable chairs.

Any specific recommendations on how to make the Newsroom a more comfortable and inviting space?
I think that is definitely one of the strengths, and I have no recommendations for this area.

What are your thoughts on the programming changes? Pros and cons of having news in the native language versus having programming mostly in English?
For many of our students the English programming is also a great change. For students who are interested in engaging with international issues and news, this offers an opportunity for them to listen and watch international programming without the language barrier. This should open up the reading room to more students. It offers

students an opportunity to learn about other parts of the world that they may not have studied in their classes even if they have studied at least one world language. Instead of being limited to one channel, they now have the opportunity to watch several channels from different corners of the world.

Did you notice your students using the radios rather than getting within proximity of the TVs to hear the programming?
It really depended on the station. There were one or two stations where they were within proximity of the tvs and others where they seemed to use the radios.

What do you think of each listening option? Is one better than the others? Last year, did you have students using headphones in the jacks?
I think the use of stations for listening is a preferred option. You are more mobile, which is nice, but a few of the students had problems with static. With the headphones in the jacks, they all had good quality of sound, but they had to cluster together, which made it more of a shared experience than an individual experience.

What specific changes did you make to the assignment?
Last year, the emphasis was really on interpreting the actions of the news presenters, looking at images and trying to discover what issues were covered and how this coverage varied from country to country. This year, they were able to watch and listen and try to discern what was covered differently in different countries and why this may be as well as what wasn't covered in some places. It was more of a specific

comparison than last year. Last year they had to draw conclusions based on what they saw versus what they heard this year.

Any specific recommendations for programming?
I thought the mixture of news and other programming was great. Is it possible to add an African station? That would be a nice addition, if possible, and it would provide students with an opportunity to learn about an area of the world where there are a lot of negative assumptions about the use of technology and communication.

Dr Whitehead's comments indicate that we were wise to remove the large library tables and increase our soft seating to create a more relaxed and comfortable atmosphere. Also, that by switching from broadcasts in foreign languages to primarily English language newsfeeds that the Newsroom would be more inclusive, rather than less so. We will also need to find a solution to provide quality audio for the televisions very soon. The radios, although inexpensive and highly portable, do not seem to provide the needed fidelity and turning up the volume any higher on the televisions would be too distracting to others in surrounding areas. This indicates that we will have to come up with a means of providing more plug-in jacks for headphones – a challenge because they require a power source and cannot be moved from location to location. In the interim, we may be able to supply the small radios to faculty and their classes who come to the Newsroom, but could not sustain the bulk cost (approximately $2.50 each) indefinitely. Although it is possible that having students clustered around a television and watching together would offer additional opportunities for shared experiences and ease of discussion, depending upon the size of the class and how many others are in the space.

If other classes wish to visit the Newsroom – and we certainly hope that by Dr Whitehead's example and word of mouth advertising they will – we will certainly require a protocol for reserving the space for class visits or at the least create signage with a schedule. Students are rather accustomed to the latter type of arrangement as this is their experience with many computer labs on campus that serve as both classroom spaces and as open labs. Dr Whitehead's assignment for her students was exactly the sort of class activity we had in mind for the International Newsroom and now that she has blazed the trail, it may provide impetus for librarians to approach their faculty and develop assignments that would encourage students to use the International Newsroom for course work and personal enrichment.

The enthusiasm exhibited over popular culture programming on some of our television channels may imply a need to rename our space, since the coverage now goes beyond exclusively news programming. We will continue to evaluate our service provider to see if there are ways to change programming quickly to accommodate specific requests. Also, we have been trying to locate a reliable and affordable package that includes broadcasts in English from the African continent, especially in light of the university's recent partnership with Moi University in Eldoret, Kenya.

In summary, our future plans to assess the usage of the International Newsroom include:

- Administer a survey to students in all classes that come to the International Newsroom. This will require a mechanism for librarians and/or faculty to alert the

Diversity Council or Reference Desk to prepare the space, post signs advising users of a class visit, and having copies of the survey available.

- Ask faculty for feedback on their class's use of the Newsroom and its resources, possibly by automatically e-mailing them a link to an online survey via Survey Monkey (University Library subscribes to this service, but there are also free versions).

- Petition the library's website editors for a link on the homepage to information about the International Newsroom, including links to the surveys, additional library resources, etc. Add a similar link to the Faculty Support page. Use the website statistics logs to determine how often these links are used.

- Offer workshops for librarians, faculty, and the Center for Teaching and Learning on how to incorporate the Newsroom into instruction, provide sample assignments or activities that exhibit how the International Newsroom can be utilized in support of campus diversity, the RISE initiative (see Chapter 4), study abroad programming, the Principles of Undergraduate Learning (see Chapter 1), and information literacy. Record the number of workshops offered, attendance at the workshops, which marketing venues used to advertise the workshops were most effective, and how many usages of the Newsroom resulted directly from the workshops.

Qualitative assessment

As useful as the information gleaned from surveys and questionnaires can be, qualitative feedback regarding the changes and impact that our diversity initiatives have made provides the richest information, particularly as reflected in the lives and work of our staff, as evidenced by the following comments from an original Diversity Council member:

> I used to be very angry at the library at the racial inequalities in hiring practices. I noticed that there were very few minority librarians, and only slightly more minority full-time non-librarian staff. I thought this was due to racism on the part of the library. Since serving on the Diversity Council, I have come to realize that it is more complicated than that. I believe now that the library wants to hire minority staff, but that for a variety of reasons, not many minority staff apply for open positions. Part of the problem is that not many minority individuals go to library school. I am pleased that this is being addressed in a profession-wide manner with scholarships and cohort programs for minorities. The Diversity Council made a small contribution to this effort with its Diversity Scholars program and perhaps also with its READ posters. I still think it is important to hire minority staff, but I have more patience with the library in its efforts now.
>
> I think my service on the Diversity Council has energized me in my day-to-day work. I have really enjoyed my service and would like to be on the council again at some point in the future. Between my work on the International Newsroom and my work putting together the GLBT grant, I feel like I've made a real contribution to diversity at the library, and that's given me a sense of pride and accomplishment.

And this from two new Council members, when asked what attracted them to serve:

> I think diversity is a most relevant issue and a major driving force in any educational institution. As a college library, our community continuously broadens to include, educate and empower individuals from many backgrounds. Their multiple talents benefit us all. The creed of UL Diversity Council mirrors my personal beliefs so I felt compelled to join it.
>
> I decided to join the council because diversity is all about celebrating individuality. And individuality is what makes people interesting. Taking part in the council seemed like a good way to help encourage students, faculty, and staff to embrace each other's differences, thereby creating a more engaged, creative, and open-minded community.

8

Challenges and opportunities to continued diversity initiatives

Abstract: This chapter discusses the current IUPUI campus climate and how it offers opportunities to continue and expand diversity initiatives in the library. Libraries can serve as models on their campus by offering ways to engage students and create an environment where they feel comfortable discussing what are often difficult and sometimes inflammatory issues.

Key words: diversity, multiculturalism, universities, academic libraries, outreach, campus climate.

Current campus climate: opportunities to make a difference

IUPUI's Office of Information Management and Institutional Research (IMIR) frequently conducts student surveys on a variety of issues, such as satisfaction with campus services or reasons for leaving the university. The results of the 2009 Student Pulse Survey (*http://survey.iupui.edu/pulse/*) – which covered a wide range of topics from cost of parking to the operating hours of the library – indicated that 'intercultural-communication and diversity on campus' was of the highest importance for the students who responded. While this result was somewhat surprising, it was the analysis of the comments made by the students that gives us pause. While we had hoped that we had made significant strides in creating a more open, diverse, and welcoming environment, the responses indicate that we still have a good deal more work to do. This also means that we are now presented with a great opportunity to pursue new ideas and continue our diversity dialogue.

The most striking aspect of the comments exhibited that most students define 'diversity' almost exclusively in terms of race, ethnicity, cultural heritage, and national origin; very few mentioned other aspects of diversity, such as ability, age, gender, gender identity, sexual orientation, or socio-economic status. Many respondents, regardless of race or ethnicity, indicated feelings of being marginalized: Caucasian and Christian students, who are the demographic majority, feel that they are overlooked as not being 'different' enough to merit special attention. Minority and international students feel that not enough is being done to support them in campus program activities, in the classroom, and financially. To us, this indicates the University Library Diversity Council and Diversity Scholars are on the right track by developing and hosting events such as Beyond Stereotypes that offer opportunities for students of all the diverse groups, not simply multicultural groups, to discuss issues of importance in a safe, non-judgmental environment. The students' comments underscore the need for us to continue the Beyond Stereotypes series and perhaps expand upon it and offer it more often. There is also great potential for developing new initiatives in partnership with other campus units, such as the Office of International Affairs and additional student organizations.

With regard to diversity-related events on campus, many students indicated that we need more of these events and that they should be better publicized. As we have encountered with library events, our students, particularly those who do not live on campus, complain that events are not scheduled at times that permit them to attend. In addition, several students suggested that rather than events to celebrate a specific ethnic group, IUPUI should offer events that encourage the interaction of all cultures. IUPUI's Office of International Affairs currently hosts an annual International Day that strives to do this. The event is widely publicized and, in good weather, held in a prominent location outdoors so there is great potential for spontaneous attendance by students who hear the music or see the booths from a distance. Unfortunately, the new campus Multicultural Center is sometimes viewed as a bastion of a single ethnic group and various student organizations are often seen as unwelcoming by those outside these specific groups. We feel that the library can also assist in these arenas by serving as a neutral space for people to interact and feel comfortable establishing inter-cultural relationships. The library is viewed as a place that doesn't 'belong' to any one group and we experience the diversity of our student population in our building on a daily basis in numerous spaces where students can study, socialize, or work in small groups. We can recruit the library's student advisory group or campus student organizations to suggest event scheduling options that may improve attendance, although we fear we are all competing for our students' attention and precious free time. This could be another signal that those of us pursuing diversity programming should pool our resources, creativity, and suggestions for a better coordinated approach to garner greater student participation. The students' comments indicated a desire for campus unity on issues of diversity; perhaps we should unify our diversity efforts to reach the students.

Many students believe a diverse campus enhances their college experience, but stressed the need to emphasize commonalities across groups rather than differences. They also raised concerns that undue attention to diversity may come at the expense of teaching or faculty quality and actually impede their education. Many find their instructors are often unaware of diversity issues, citing language barriers (actual and perceived), and lack of tolerance or respect for diverse student populations. These comments provide clues to ways we can help increase awareness of diversity issues among the faculty by building on our current librarian/faculty relationships and expanding those collaborations beyond one-shot bibliographic instruction sessions and collection development budgetary concerns. Successful connections between the library and students are often based upon first establishing the library's value and importance among the faculty. University Library's International Newsroom could serve as an excellent setting for course-based information literacy sessions that expose instructors and students to new sources of information and different points of view. This may be especially attractive to many junior faculty who are eager to experiment with new ways to engage students and provide alternative learning experiences beyond traditional lectures.

Diversity initiatives require administrative support

Since the campus administration considers diversity to be a major focus, it can be assumed that other units on campus will follow suit, including the libraries. But such initiatives go nowhere without campus support, generally in the form of a diversity officer and occasionally with modest sums of money. In academic libraries, these efforts falter without the wholehearted backing of the library's Dean or Director and support of a dedicated administrative team. While many units on our campus have created diversity committees or councils, their efforts seem to center on recruitment (students and faculty) and do little regarding outreach or awareness programs. This presents academic libraries with a unique opportunity to be a leader on campus by creating a model for other units, increasing the library's value to the university, supporting the university's mission and vision, and furthering the library's own mission and vision.

Academic libraries worldwide face shrinking budgets and reduced purchasing power and often 'extras' suffer, such as our Undergraduate Diversity Scholar Program, which had originally been two part-time hourly student positions. In light of probable budget cuts and using the recent student survey, the Diversity Council made recommendations to the Dean of the Library that we continue the Diversity Scholar program with one Scholar rather than two, and not provide a stipend or release time to the Scholar's supervisor. Since the supervisory responsibilities are additional duties for a full-time librarian, we had experienced difficulties finding someone willing to accept this role from year-to-year due to the increased workload that the position entails. The Dean was able to earmark funds to maintain a single Scholar for the coming year and supervisory responsibilities have been spread around to 'project leaders', which allows the Diversity Scholar to engage with multiple teams and individuals in the library. One librarian maintains a mentoring relationship with the Scholar as a central facilitator.

Issues of bureaucratic red tape

Another challenge to establishing diversity initiatives in academic libraries is the inherent bureaucracy and red tape found in many universities. This was especially evident when our Diversity Scholar, Autumn, proposed sending computers to Southern University of New Orleans. It involved multiple campus departments, paperwork, and signatures. Other projects, such as 'To Mexico With Love' with Diversity Scholars Trina and Ashley, were handled more expeditiously and in-house. Often this bureaucracy is something that simply needs to be tolerated or overcome with improved planning, particularly when it comes to locating funding sources. IUPUI makes some funding available for diversity projects and initiatives, but we have also discovered grant sources at the unit level, such as the GLBT Faculty Staff Council grant we pursued for a special event and to develop the library's GLBT collection of DVDs. Bureaucracy can also be, if not avoided, at least ameliorated by locating the proper contact person within a unit who will respond quickly and offer guidance. Pursuing and nurturing networks on campus not only helps obtain funds and information, but makes others aware of the library's goals, projects, and events.

Ability to move quickly

Speed and agility is often needed to act on unexpected opportunities, particularly when writing grants for project funding. The Diversity Council often doesn't hear about grant opportunities until the last moment, or the grants have short lead times. But we discovered that the more grants we wrote, the better and quicker we got at it, even when 'writing by committee'. A natural lead grant writer often emerged, often the person who had first learned of it and suggested the Council pursue it, or another committee member who had a passion for the specific topic or event. Occasionally we learned that there are no short cuts and we regretfully had to allow some opportunities to pass, but we always learned from our experiences and gained more confidence and expertise to prepare for the next prospect.

Lack of campus coordination

We find our efforts to coordinate activities with other units on campus difficult due to a lack of knowledge and interaction with other campus diversity groups. Although the IUPUI Office of Diversity, Equity, and Inclusion (ODEI) has a substantial website (*http://diversity.iupui.edu/*)it does not serve as a practical central clearing house to locate resources and grant opportunities, share ideas for cross-campus events and projects, or publicity. What University Library *can* do is ensure our Diversity Council is mentioned on the OEDI website and communicate regularly with this office's Director of Multicultural Academic Relations. We can suggest ways to share projects and co-develop events, raise the library's profile on diversity issues, and prove our value to the University. The work performed to date by our Diversity Council and Scholars has already opened doors among student groups and other units on campus, so we have established a solid foundation upon which we can continue to build. We may someday take the step of creating a position for a Diversity Librarian. This type of appointment is becoming more common among US academic libraries, generally as means of diversifying the library's workforce. We would certainly expand that role to encompass our current outreach and programming activities.

Spreading our message

IUPUI enjoys a plethora of campus communication tools, including campus e-mail, school and departmental listservs, and the *JagNews* online campus-wide newsletter, which is pushed via campus e-mails twice a week, but severely limits the amount of text permitted for each announcement. There is also an online event calendar and designated locations on campus for approved posters and flyers. Unfortunately, students tend to pay scant attention to campus e-mail, often ignore their school listservs (which use the campus e-mail system), ignore or opt out of *JagNews*, and generally do not make the effort to visit the event calendar unless they're searching for a specific activity that will garner 'extra credit' for a course grade. The university also has a very rich campus website, but in the jostling for front page real estate, even the Office of Diversity, Equity & Inclusion lacks the status to merit a top-level link. Our challenge has been to cut through the 'noise' generated by these myriad communications and ensure that our students, faculty, and staff are aware of University Library's diversity initiatives and outreach events. Since campus marketing outlets have yielded limited results, we have tried to find other ways to promote ourselves.

We have had some success by advertising events on the News & Events page of the library's website and pushing stories via *Gateway*, the library's electronic newsletter. Our subject librarians have also contributed by forwarding our marketing e-mails to their schools and departments for distribution to students and the teaching faculty. Librarians have also assisted by making announcements while performing instruction in classrooms, giving library tours, and posting notices in the university's online course management systems during first year seminar courses, with which we have been involved for many years. Achieving buy-in from faculty is perhaps the most effective method of reaching the students. This was instrumental to the success of the Beyond Stereotypes events in 2009 as a few faculty encouraged their students to attend and, in one case, brought his class to the event site. The Diversity Council and Scholars have also tapped into the growing number of social networking tools, such as Facebook, Twitter, and weblogs to promote programs, exhibits, and events (LinkedIn, Hyves, Tuenti, Skyrock, Hi5, etc., can be used for this purpose as well).

But our most successful means of making our constituencies aware of our diversity programming and resources has been old-fashioned word-of-mouth. Our most recent group of Diversity Scholar applicants all indicated that they had heard about the Undergraduate Diversity Scholar Program from current or former Scholars. We plan to capitalize on this strategy by contacting campus groups, such as the O Team (upperclassmen who conduct orientation for incoming students), to schedule brief presentations about the Scholar Program, indicate where to find application materials, describe upcoming events, and suggest library materials related to diversity. The Diversity Council has also decided to develop specialized online research guides about diversity topics, beginning with a gay/lesbian/bisexual/transgender (GLBT) guide, and will be digitizing unique library resources on the history of the campus, which was built on what was, historically, primarily an African American neighborhood. We anticipate that short videos made available through a variety of venues (the library's website, Facebook, YouTube, and the campus website) will increasingly be used to promote our outreach as well.

Engaging students and staff

The primary goal of our diversity outreach and programming has always been to engage our students with the library. We have worked most effectively with campus student organizations through our young Diversity Scholars. Although University Library has made inroads by interacting with students directly, for example by conducting surveys or recruiting a student advisory group, we have found that students are always more willing to interact with other students. These peer to peer interactions have proven to be especially rich and valuable. It is always challenging to find the 'perfect' time to schedule programming that will ensure strong attendance, particularly by students at an urban, commuter campus. Whenever possible, we schedule an event for two dates and times to give the attendees an alternative opportunity to attend.

Another goal of our outreach has been to engage the library staff. We have been fully cognizant of the need to alleviate concerns and resistance inherent in any new initiative, particularly ones that may have emotional implications for some. Again, our Diversity Scholars have been instrumental in building bridges. The Scholars have desks and computers in an open cubicle area of the library that houses support staff, such as cataloging, interlibrary loan, and technology support and are able to meet and greet staff as they walk to and from their desks. The Scholars have also been working with multiple library teams and have taken advantage of these relationships to foster real change on a one-to-one level. The students' enthusiasm has been infectious and they have requested staff input and assistance with displays and events. Perhaps the single greatest barrier to staff participation in diversity outreach and programming has simply been time. It is difficult to attend events during work hours – hourly staff members require supervisor permission to attend events during normal work hours, while faculty librarians have more freedom in this area – and events after work hours are also problematical due to family and other commitments. Generally, supervisors grant release time to staff for library initiatives, provided entire departments are not decimated at crucial service times. This is an additional advantage to scheduling events at multiple dates and times whenever possible.

Developing attractive activities and events

Our greatest challenge is to develop ideas for projects, exhibits, and events that will be attractive to the students and also help them learn about the library and what twenty-first century librarians do. We have had great success with the following:

- Trained Scholars to digitize diversity-related scholarly and archived materials in the library and print these materials for displays and online presentations.

- Partnered with campus departments and student groups to create exhibits that raise awareness about the library and its resources that support diversity at the university.

- Used American Library Association (ALA) software packages to design, create, and display personalized

READ posters that celebrate the diversity of library staff. The posters are displayed throughout the library and appear on the library's website.

- Recorded oral histories of faculty, staff, students and members of the local community from diverse backgrounds and made them available online.

- Partnered with the IUPUI Office of International Affairs' annual International Festival. University Library librarians staffed a table with games, information on resources, and free giveaway items.

- Developed a film series using DVDs owned by the library (with public presentation rights) and follow-up discussions with speakers from the local community.

We plan to expand our outreach activities, despite mounting budget constraints and other pressing concerns. We feel that diversity issues will continue to be of great importance to our students, and therefore our campus. University Library can continue to contribute to IUPUI's commitment to diversity and perhaps even be a model to other units on our campus.

We invite our many dedicated colleagues from other libraries to share their experiences with diversity outreach and programming so we may learn from each other to enrich ourselves and our students' experiences.

Appendix A

IUPUI University Library Strategic Plan for Diversity 2007–2009

Prepared by the IUPUI University Library Diversity Council

Diversity Goal 1: Recruitment, academic achievement, persistence and graduation of a diverse student body

1.1 Diversity Undergraduate Scholars Program

Establish a Diversity Undergraduate Scholars Program, whose applicants are from populations underrepresented in library professionals/staff. The program will mimic the structure of SLIS graduate assistantships, meaning the fellow could participate in work for various library Teams, supervised by that Team's leader. Additionally the fellow will participate in organizing University Library's monthly multicultural displays (see goal 3.2). This fellow will be appointed for a full academic year. Expected hours per week is 20 and expected compensation is $10 per hour.

The hope of this program is to not only increase the diversity of our student worker population but also serves as a means of introducing the work of libraries or librarianship as a career to individuals who may not have otherwise considered this work, which also helps to reach Diversity Goal 2 of recruiting and retaining diverse faculty and staff.

As part of the application process the applicant will be asked to define multicultural and describe how he/she embodies this concept.

It is important that this program be open to students of all age, ability, cultural heritage, ethnic background, gender, gender identity, national origin, race, religion, sexual orientation, and socioeconomic status.

Goal Follow-up: 1.1 Diversity Undergraduate Scholars Program

In late Summer 2007 the Diversity Council advertised for the IUPUI University Library Diversity Undergraduate Scholars Program. The goals of the program included:

- Increase the diversity of the University Library Staff
- Hire individuals with a commitment to and belief in the positive effects of diversity in the workplace
- Give undergraduates the opportunity to do professional level work in a library setting, providing insight into a career that may not have otherwise been considered
- Endow undergraduates with skills transferable to any career.

We had a tremendous response with over 20 applicants. Four undergraduates were interviewed and two selected. Projects in which the Scholars have been involved include:

- Uploading scholarly works into digital archives
- Creating metadata for scholarly works
- Utilizing software tools such as Photoshop, Open Journal System, and DSpace
- Researching and posting regular displays related to diversity
- Connecting with student groups regarding library and research related issues
- Raising funds for a local middle school library through organization of a Scholastic Book Fair
- Maintaining regular postings on the IUPUI University Library Diversity Scholars Blog
- Attending University Library Board Meetings
- Attending Indiana State Library Diversity Council Meetings
- Recording and transcribing an oral history with a former IUPUI faculty member
- Assembling and organizing a book collection, and conducting

user education for a library at women's shelter in Mexico in collaboration with the IUPUI *To Mexico with Love Program*

- Designing posters for the University Library READ poster campaign.

The Council considers the Diversity Undergraduate Scholars Program to be one of our most significant accomplishments with evidence of impact demonstrated through an Institute for Museum and Library Services grant that was applied for by the Indiana State Library. This grant is centered around increasing the diversity of Indiana libraries' employees and bases some of its proposal on the IUPUI University Library Diversity Undergraduate Scholars Program.

New Goal 1.2: Provide copies of *The Indianapolis Recorder* free to IUPUI students

The library now has a weekly bulk subscription to the local, nationally recognized Black newspaper, *The Indianapolis Recorder* and places the free copies in the same area as other free periodical publications. Additionally the library has suggested to campus administration that this free access be extended to other locations on campus.

Diversity Goal 2: Recruit, retain, advance, recognize, and promote a diverse faculty, staff and administration while creating a campus-wide community that celebrates its own diversity as one of its strengths and as a means of shaping IUPUI's identity as a university

2.1 Recruiting and Hiring Diverse Library Employees

For fiscal year 2008, 25 percent of the total new University Library hires at the levels of PA, Clerical, Faculty, and TE should be from populations underrepresented in library professionals/staff.

Goal Follow-up: 2.1 Recruiting and Hiring Diverse Library Employees

The Council has been communicating with Library Human Resources librarian Mary Stanley regarding our current job posting practices. The council has compiled a list of suggested job posting locales for increasing the diversity of the pool of applicants for open positions.

2.2 Diverse Librarian/Library Staff Posters/Media

Create and post posters, bookmarks, and/or other media that illustrate the multicultural background of librarians and library staff. Similarly to nurse recruitment campaigns, we will open people's eyes to librarianship/library work as a career by visually presenting people from a variety of cultures working in libraries. If individuals are agreeable we could use University Library staff members in the posters which would add another level of meaning for viewers, the person in the poster would not just be a face but someone they can actually speak to in University Library.

Additionally these posters (either the actual printed poster or just the file) could be made either freely available or made available for purchase.

Nursing campaign examples:

http://www.jnj.com/images/content/content_images/2002 AnnualReport/review/nurse.jpg

http://www.oregoncenterfornursing.org/documents/poster_67k.jpg

Goal Follow-up: 2.2 Diverse Librarian/Library Staff Posters/ Media

In collaboration with the Teaching, Learning, and Research Team Marketing Group a READ poster campaign is currently underway. These posters will display library holding their favorite books and include a job description. The hope is that students and other library users will find staff more approachable as a result of being able to put a name with the face. Additionally we believe that showing the diversity of the library staff and diversity of the type of work that occurs in libraries will also be of benefit to the library and its users.

Diversity Goal 3: Make diversity a strategic priority touching all aspects of the campus mission

3.1 Multicultural Materials Fund

Establish a budget/fund for multicultural materials for purposeful collection of material, both print and electronic, that 'reflect[s] the full diversity of the human experience and commentary on it' (from the objective under IUPUI Diversity Goal 3 about the library collections). Encourage liaisons that are already purchasing multicultural materials to continue doing so. This new fund will be used for purchasing additional, more unique multicultural items that may not have been attained with subject-based funds. Funds will also support multicultural material purchases for the Herron Art Library.

Goal Follow-up: 3.1 Multicultural Materials Fund

The Collection Development Working Group rejected this proposal for setting aside funds specifically for the development of multicultural material. Instead CDCG recommended that all librarians continue the practice of purchasing diversity related materials with current subject based funds.

3.2 Monthly Multicultural Displays

Enhance climate for multiculturalism through the creation of monthly displays following the various nationally recognized, month-long multicultural celebrations, e.g. Martin Luther King Jr. day (January), Black History Month (Feb), Women's History Month (March), Asian/Pacific American Heritage Month (May), Gay/Lesbian/Bisexual/Transgendered Pride month (June), Anniversary of Americans with Disabilities Act (July 26), Hispanic Heritage Month (Sept 15–Oct 15).

The creation of these displays will be an important opportunity for all members of University Library staff to become involved in increasing their own and others' awareness of many cultures and points of view. Staff should attend a diversity training session (to occur during Organization Week) prior to display creation. Prior to University Library's Organization Week each year each staff member will be randomly appointed to one of twelve display groups. Each group will have a designated leader. During Organization Week each of the twelve groups will have time to meet, develop the concept for their display, and begin working on the assembly of the display. Each group will install their month's display no more than four days into their appointed month.

Each group should consider consulting campus student groups, faculty groups, and library liaisons which pertain to their topic for ideas. For the first year of displays, each month's team will be responsible for all display creation, set-up, and tear down of their month's display. Once hired the Multicultural Undergraduate Fellow (see Goal 1) will participate in display creation for every month and will be responsible for uninstalling the previous month's display in addition to various other tasks.

Goal Follow-up: 3.2 Monthly Multicultural Displays

While the displays have not been monthly they have been regular. These displays are created by the Diversity Fellows and thus far have been housed in the display cases in the Café area of University Library. They have included topics such as Black History Month: highlighting the historic IUPUI neighborhood, GLBT Awareness month: highlighting student activist groups on campus as well as prominent GLBT scholars and artists, and finally Native American Indian Heritage Month which also highlighted related student groups on campus. These displays have not only been successful in creating a more welcoming and thoughtful environment in the lower level of the library but have also given the library the opportunity to connect with student groups on campus.

Diversity Goal 4: Regularly assess, evaluate, improve and communicate diversity efforts of IUPUI

4.1 Assessment of Existing Data

University Library has conducted an annual user survey since 1999. The objectives of the survey include: Identifying categories of service that library patrons seek and use; Identifying who our customers are; Obtaining a general picture of the quality of library service; and obtaining a baseline data set which would prove useful in identifying areas in need of attention. From this data the library already has a snapshot of various aspects of diversity as related to library users. For example, the data shows that between 1999 and 2003 an average of 26 percent of the library's users were observed to be minorities, 53 percent male, 47 percent female, and 12 percent spoke English as a second language.

While we have survey data regarding University Library users we have yet to conduct an in-depth, multivariate analysis with regards to diversity. Because we will be using already existing data that was not specifically collected for diversity analysis purposes, the library's initial diversity assessment goal is to develop a plan detailing the process by which existing data can be used to evaluate

University Library's state of diversity. This plan should include identification of:

- Specific pieces of data that will be compared/contrasted/analyzed
- Surveys/years that will be examined
- How and by whom the data will analyzed
- Cost of analysis
- How and by whom the data sets will be regularized/converted to a like format (if needed).

Goal Follow-up: 4.1 Assessment of Existing Data

This goal involved analyzing survey data collected over the past few years regarding how users spend their time while in the library. Survey data analyzation has not yet occurred.

New Goal: 4.2 Compile a list of IUPUI courses with diversity related components and assess whether library collections and instruction are currently meeting the needs of these courses

This project will be completed by the 2008/2009 Diversity Fellows and led by a Librarian.

New Goal: 4.3 Complete a literature review for conducting a collection assessment based on diversity

The Diversity Council is currently working on this literature review to pass along to the Collection Development Group.

Updated December 15, 2009

Appendix B

IUPUI University Library Diversity Council Charter

Prepared by the IUPUI University Library Diversity Council

Based on Yale University Library's Diversity Strategic Plan 2006–2008 *http://www.library.yale.edu/lhr/diversity/ YULDC%20Strategic%20Plan.pdf*

IUPUI University Library Diversity Strategic Plan 2010–2011

Purpose and Vision

Indiana University and IUPUI have long held commitments to diversity. The Indiana University Board of Trustees statement of the University's Objectives and Ideals states, in part, that 'Indiana University is committed to the principle of equal educational and occupational opportunities for all persons and to positive action toward elimination of discrimination in all phases of University life, as set forth in the Indiana University Affirmative Action Plan.' (June 29, 1974, Indiana University Academic Handbook, 1992, p. 2, Appendix F.) In 2006, IUPUI Chancellor Charles R. Bantz renewed this commitment and reinvigorated IUPUI's actions towards the end of making the IUPUI population more representative of our globally diverse community and making IUPUI's climate welcoming for all students, employees, and visitors. In the Fall of 2007 Chancellor Bantz called for the formation of departmental

Diversity Councils whose responsibility it is to create departmental level diversity strategies, initiatives, and goals that aid in reaching the campus-wide IUPUI Diversity Vision, Mission, Values & Goals (*http://www.iupui.edu/diversity/vision.html*). This document represents IUPUI University Library's Diversity Council's work in support of IUPUI's Diversity Vision, Mission, Values & Goals.

The Diversity Council's (hereinafter referred to as The Council) overarching goals are to enhance the diversity and cultural competence of our staff so that our workplace continues to evolve into an even more inclusive and congenial environment. This type of atmosphere is conducive to job satisfaction and will in turn lead to even more effective service to our diverse patrons. Additionally we support the increase of the library's efforts towards being a more inviting place for all our users including university students, faculty, staff, and community members.

The Council recognizes various attributes relating to diversity including, but not limited to, ability, age, cultural heritage, ethnic background, gender, gender identity, national origin, race, religion, sexual orientation, and socio-economic status. Embracing diversity is a key component of excellence in the workplace that allows individuals to reach their full potential. The Council strives to provide a positive work and learning environment which is free of any form of bigotry, harassment, intimidation, threat, or abuse, whether verbal or written, physical or psychological, direct or implied. The Council views multiculturalism and pluralism as essential components of its mission and work.

Charter and Structure

Purpose

The Council was formed to enhance the diversity and cultural competence of our employees as well as to create an atmosphere that is supportive of diverse populations and scholarly activity reflecting diverse populations. Ultimately this leads to a work environment more conducive to job satisfaction and a collection of facilities, research resources, and research assistance that more effectively serves our diverse patrons.

Overall Goals

- Recommend strategic actions, initiatives, and goals to be taken by University Library to reach IUPUI's Diversity Vision, Mission, Values & Goals.
- Evaluate the outcomes of each strategic action, initiative, or goal on an annual basis.
- Recommend revisions to strategic actions, initiatives, and goals based on annual evaluation.

Regular Duty

- Solicit applications for the following year's Diversity Undergraduate Scholars Program and select the following year's Scholar(s).

Sponsor

The sponsor of The Council is the Dean of IUPUI University Library.

Membership

The Council is comprised of 5–10 members consisting of:

- 2–3 University Library Faculty Organization (ULFO) members (not including ex officio members of the Diversity Council)
- 2–3 University Library Staff Group (ULSG) members
- The Dean of IUPUI University Library is an ex officio member to whom term limits do not apply
- The past chair is an ex officio member for 1 year following chairship.

Members are elected for a term of 2 years, serving no more than 2 consecutive terms. Preferably, 1/3 to 1/2 of the committee members will be a carry-over from the previous committee. It is suggested but not required that at least 1, but no more than 3, IUPUI University Library student employee(s) be sought for service on the Diversity Council.

Quorum

2/3 of The Council members constitutes a quorum.

Officers

The Council elects a Chair and Secretary.

Duties of the Chair

- Primarily to call and chair the meetings
- Ensure that all members of The Council have the opportunity to be heard on all issues
- Run the affairs of The Council
- When necessary, poll the members for opinions
- Appoint student employees to The Council
- Ensure that The Council members are elected via ULFO and ULSG in a timely manner
- Update the IUPUI University Library Strategic Plan for Diversity document as needed
- Ensure that the Council has solicited applications for the following year's Diversity Undergraduate Scholars Program and that the following year's Scholar(s) have been selected.

Duties of the Secretary

- Record, distribute to The Council (and others as needed), and maintain archive of the Council's meeting minutes
- Maintain a list of current and past members of The Council
- Request updates to the e-mail Exchange group IN-ULIB-DIVERSITY as needed
- Maintain The Council's web presence.

Elections

Members

The Council's members from ULFO and ULSG are elected by each respective organization, according to that organization's guidelines for electing representatives to other bodies.

Student committee members may be proposed by any University Library employee but are appointed by the Chair of The Council.

Membership terms run from date of election in June–May 31.

Officers

Officer terms last 1 year. Officers each serve no more than 2 consecutive 1-year terms in the same office. The Chair must be a ULFO or ULSG member. Officers are nominated by any member of The Council during the first Council meeting in June, which is called to order by the Past Chair. A quorum of Council members is required for electing officers. Officers are elected by secret ballot by The Council.

Officer terms run from date of election in June–May 31.

In the event that the Chair relinquishes his/her position prior to the expiration of his/her term the Dean of University Library, considering input and suggestions from The Council, may appoint a replacement to complete the relinquished Chair's term.

Frequency of meetings

The Council shall meet at least 4 times a year.

Meeting Norms and Ground Rules

- Arrive on time
- Begin promptly
- End promptly
- Meet your deadlines
- Be accountable
- Stay goal oriented – time is a scarce resource
- Be fully present and participatory
- Be open and honest
- Respect each other's views
- Every idea is important
- Minority opinions are important
- Disagreement is acceptable

- Try to resolve individual disagreements with individual member first; then go to Chair if needed
- Maintain confidentiality of sensitive topics
- Absolutely no disrespectful behavior.

Modifications

Modifications to this Charter and Structure may be proposed by any University Library employee. A quorum of The Council is required for voting on modifications to the Charter and Structure.

Proposed modifications may be discussed prior to a meeting of The Council and must be discussed at a meeting of The Council prior to voting. Decisions regarding modifications are reached via a secret ballot vote by The Council. A proposal is passed if 2/3 majority vote is reached.

Updated June 4, 2010

Appendix C

University Library Undergraduate Diversity Scholar Supervisor Position Description
Updated June 15, 2010

Summary

The Diversity Scholar Supervisor will be a University Library librarian and a member of the University Library Diversity Council.* The Supervisor will be the Scholar's primary contact within University Library. While the Scholar may be working with other Teams and Team representatives, and therefore be trained or supervised in project-specific tasks, the Diversity Scholar Supervisor remains responsible for the Scholar's overall work experience as a University Library Undergraduate Diversity Scholar. The Supervisor is selected by the Dean of University Library and may serve no more than 2 consecutive 1-year terms.

Required Tasks

- Participate in the Scholar's selection and interview process
- Orient the Scholar to the library staff, building, and policies

* Nomination and election to the Diversity Council occurs through the University Library Specialists Group (ULSG) and University Library Faculty Organization (ULFO). If the Diversity Scholar Supervisor is not already an elected member of the Diversity Council, he/she becomes an ex officio member. See IUPUI University Library Diversity Council Charter and Structure *http://www.ulib.iupui.edu/about/diversity/plan#structure.*

- Arrange for the Scholar's workspace, keys, and card entry as necessary
- Meet on a weekly basis with the Scholar to ensure all assigned tasks are being met and answer any questions
- Review, edit as necessary, and approve the Scholar's time sheet
- Facilitate the Scholar's interaction with other University Library Teams, including coordinating a time schedule to ensure smooth and continuous workflow for the Scholar and the Teams
- Monitor the Scholar Program budget, making workflow adjustments as needed
- Ensure that the University Library Diversity Scholar Supervisor for the following year has been identified and nominated for the position.
- Develop/Coordinate the development of (in conjunction with the University Library Diversity Council and other library Teams) the tasks and projects in which the following year's Scholar will participate
- Evaluate the Scholar's performance prior to the conclusion
- Solicit feedback from the Scholar about their experience with the Diversity Scholar Program.

Appendix D

IUPUI University Library Diversity Scholars Orientation Schedule

Monday, August 18th (9 a.m.–4 p.m.) – 7 hours

Time	Activity
9:00–10:30	Welcome to University Library! Let's get acquainted! *We will meet you at the 2nd floor Reference Desk at 9:00am* Stop over your work area; verify computer and printer connections Overview of the Program, library procedures, policies, listservs
10:30–10:45	Break
10:45–11:45	Library tour • Visit all areas of the building, including 'behind the scenes' departments • Meet other library staff; learn more about our technical support services
11:45–1:15	Lunch with last year's Scholars (It's our treat–and it's on the clock!)
1:30–2:30	Meet other librarians
2:30–2:45	Break

2:45–4:00	Return to work area to arrange your work space, discuss day's activities, ask questions **Things to do for tomorrow:** 1. **Decide what days/times you want to work during the fall semester.** There should be one common day where you both are in the office so we can meet as a group. 2. **Brainstorm themes you might like to use for an exhibit in the 1st floor lobby display cases.** Upcoming celebrations include Hispanic Heritage Month (Sept. 15 – Oct. 15) and GLBT History Month (Oct.). There are two display cases, so you can do two different themes if you'd like.

Tuesday, August 19th (9 a.m.–4:30 p.m.) – 6.5 hours

Time	Activity
9:00–9:45	Set schedules for fall semester; decide on weekly meeting day Any questions since yesterday? Do you need any office supplies?
9:45–10:00	Break
10:00–11:00	Meet with staff from Special Collections and Archives to learn how they create library displays, work with Archives photos and documents, and other tips.
11:00–12:00	Discuss exhibit theme ideas you brainstormed yesterday
12:00–1:00	Lunch on your own (Don't forget to clock out and then back in again!)
1:00–2:00	Training session: working with the library's website software, Drupal
2:00–2:15	Break
2:15–4:30	Return to work area to discuss day's activities, ask questions, practice with website software Time to chat and work on 'to do' items below **Things to do for Friday:** 1. **Decide on your final exhibit theme(s).** Think about materials you may wish to use and possible library resources to highlight. 2. **Write a draft of a brief autobiography to place on University Library's website** 3. **Read over last year's Diversity Scholars' web pages and blog**

Friday, August 22nd (9 a.m.–4:30 p.m.) – 6.5 hours*

Time	Activity
9:00–10:30	Start fleshing out exhibit theme idea(s) and list of materials needed – you may wish to take measurements of the display cases, sketch out your ideas, list library staff to contact, look up books or locate online resources, locate campus resources, etc.
10:30–12:00	Meet in your work area with supervisor to review some University Library projects that will involve you. Discuss two in-depth projects that will be spearheaded by other librarians.
12:00–1:00	Lunch on your own (Don't forget to clock out and then back in again!)
1:00–2:30	Meet with Mindy Cooper at the Reference Desk to: • Learn more about some of the library's online article databases and other resources. • Specify if there are resources you may need to learn about for your first exhibit theme(s).
2:30–4:00	Write final autobiography for webpage Practice with website software and add your autobiography
4:00–4:30	End of day discussion/question time

* There is plenty of "wriggle room" built into the day today. Please feel free to take a break as needed.

Appendix E

IUPUI University Library Diversity Scholar Info Sheet

Contact Information

Please be sure to let your supervisor know if you're unable to report for work or are running more than 10 or 15 minutes late. Robin Crumrin, UL 1112F, 278-2327, rcrumrin@iupui.edu

Work Hours

UL 1115 is a restricted area of the library and is generally open Monday through Friday, 8 a.m. to 5 p.m. (excluding holidays and other exceptions). We ask that you confine your work hours to weekdays between 8 a.m. to 5 p.m. whenever possible. If it becomes necessary to work outside these hours (e.g. working until 6 p.m. to complete a work-related project), please contact your supervisor(s) to make arrangements for access to UL 1115. For safety reasons, student employees should not be in the library when the building is closed.

Computer Use

Your assigned computer is primarily for work purposes; however, you are welcome to use your work area and computer for academic purposes outside of work hours during the days and hours indicated above.

Pay Periods

Hourly employees are paid bi-weekly, every other Friday. Pay advices are posted to OneStart. Changes of name, address or tax exemptions must be made through the library's Business Administration Office (UL 1110).

Breaks/Lunch

- University employees are guaranteed one unpaid 30 minute lunch period if scheduled to work more than 6 consecutive hours. If you are working for more than 6½ consecutive hours, you are required to take a 30 minute unpaid lunch break.
- University employees are guaranteed one paid 15 minute break for every 4 consecutive hours worked.
- Paid breaks last 15 minutes and you are required to use the Take a Break from Work function on T.I.M.E.
- You must clock out for breaks longer than 15 minutes.

Use of Telephones

Cell phone reception in UL 1115 is generally poor, so you may need to step out into the lobby or outside to take or make personal calls. Student work areas aren't equipped with phones, so if you need to make work-related calls, you're welcome to use the phone in the conference room (UL 1115N), if the room is unoccupied, or let one of your supervisors know and they can make arrangements for you.

Food and Drink

Food and drinks are permitted in your work area in UL 1115. You will also receive a key to the Staff Lounge (UL 1102), which is available to all employees in the building for breaks and meals. The Staff Lounge contains vending machines, a refrigerator where you may store your food, a sink, and two microwaves. (The Staff Lounge is cleaned every Thursday and anything left in the refrigerator must be removed or labeled with your name and the date to ensure it's not thrown away.)

Visiting with Friends

Since UL 1115 is a restricted area, there should be minimal visiting with friends while you are working. Visits with friends should be limited to a few minutes and, should it become necessary to spend extra time, it would be appropriate to take a break. Frequent visits are not encouraged.

Building Closings

The university generally does not close because of adverse weather, and the library generally follows the lead of the university. If weather or other conditions are widespread and severe, such as the recent loss of air conditioning on campus, the Chancellor may cancel classes. The cancellation will be announced by means of local radio and TV stations. Be aware, however, that the cancellation of classes does not necessarily mean the campus buildings and services are closed; that is a separate action taken by the Chancellor and will be indicated in announcements. Updates are posted online at the IUPUI campus homepage at http://www.iupui.edu/.

It's also a very good idea to update your Emergency Contact Information in OneStart if you haven't done so already (see http://www.iupui.edu/~prepared/informed/ for information and instructions).

Supply Requisitions and Equipment Use

If you require office supplies, materials for projects, or access to equipment (e.g. digital camera, lamination machine, etc.), please notify your supervisors. We are trying to track supply and equipment consumption and use to help us better determine budget needs for continuing the Diversity Undergraduate Scholar Program

We're glad you're here!

Appendix F

University Library Undergraduate Diversity Scholar Program September 15, 2009

*Proposal for Resource Assistance
Project: Southern University
of New Orleans*

Summary

Part of the Diversity Scholars program is to promote and raise awareness of diversity. After viewing previous diversity projects and in correlation with my field of study, I feel compelled to embark on a service oriented project that will raise awareness of diverse issues of inequality and the ongoing need to provide support for struggling populations in our country.

I have identified a university library that is still in need of many resources after Hurricane Katrina. Southern University of New Orleans is an historically Black college that suffered great damage from the hurricane. Their library was completely destroyed and they have yet to be moved into a permanent facility.

My goal is to gather resources for SUNO library by way of fundraising projects, grant writing, and organizing a donation drive. I hope to assist SUNO in providing the academic resources that their students need in order to succeed.

I believe this is an excellent opportunity to promote University Library and its commitment to diversity. This project will also give me an opportunity to learn invaluable research and grant writing skills. I may also have an opportunity to present our work at a library conference.

Introduction

Founded in 1959, Southern University, New Orleans, is an historically black college in New Orleans, Louisiana. Hurricane Katrina has had a profound effect on this university. Four years later, this campus is still suffering from the aftermath of Katrina. Following is a summary of information regarding the effects Katrina had on their library found on SUNO's website:

> The library's mission is to support the curricular and research needs of the university community through the development of pertinent collections and the provision of services designed to facilitate access to information. SUNO Library has been unable to honor this mission since Hurricane Katrina. The library collection as well as the building itself has been destroyed. The library remains housed in trailers pending renovation of the original facility.
>
> SUNO Library's goals of enhancing the Library Academic Research Infrastructure consist of focusing on, 'the building of a highly selective core collection of physical resources, the development of a more comprehensive virtual library, and the bibliographic instruction and support needed by a university community which is increasingly composed of distance education Internet-only students and faculty.'
>
> -Mrs Shatiqua Mosby-Wilson
> *http://www.suno.edu/TitleIII/Library.html*

Needs/Problems

- SUNO's University Library has been relocated to 2 trailers and they are now expanding into a third trailer.
- Students have very limited access to library resources:
  1. Limited space has hindered them from collecting or shelving books
  2. Lack of equipment and study areas
  3. Majority of research resources have been transferred to electronic format.

- Expressed needs:

  1. Computers: preferably laptops since they have limited space (Mrs Mosby-Wilson mentioned the idea of a mobile lab so that hey can open up space for study carrels).

- Equipment to set up a Smart classroom:

  1. Projectors: Mrs Mosby-Wilson mentioned that a professor came looking for a projector and she could not provide it.

- Traditional transparency and Portable projectors:

  1. Electronic Documents: due to limited space, most of SUNO's library materials have been converted to digital format. We could get a list from them of documents they are in need of, and scan them or transfer files we may already have scanned in.

     a. Kindle e-book readers: would be useful since the majority of their material is in electronic format.

     b. Books: Mrs Mosby-Wilson did say that there are some books that they do want to replace for the students.

        i. She suggested that if we do a Scholastic Book fair, instead of donating the money to SUNO library, Scholastic gives 1.5 credits per dollar for the purchasing of books.

        ii. If Scholastic does not provide the college level books, the money collected could still be used for the purchase of equipment.

     c. DVD players.

     d. Portable white screen.

Goals and Objectives

- Fundraising events coordinated by us for SUNO

  1. Scholastic Book Fair

  2. Grant research and writing

  3. Gather resources that may be donated from IUPUI as well as other businesses.

- Travel to the university by our Diversity Scholars to deliver materials/funds personally

  1. Meet the people we are collaborating with

  2. Possible presentation on the project.

- Collaboration with SUNO's Library Director, Shatiqua Mosby-Wilson, in collection of data and development of a formal presentation that could later be presented at ALA, ACRL or other Library Conference.

    1. The goals of the conference presentation would be to increase awareness of SUNO's ongoing issues, as well as present our efforts to assist them.

    2. Mrs Mosby-Wilson mentioned that their library was interested in presenting information on how they are managing their assistance/donation resources at the conference as well.

Timetable

	Description of Work	Start and End Dates
Phase One	Project approval: complete	09/15/09–09/25/09
Phase Two	Gather Data/Information on resources needed at library: complete	9/25/09–10/15/09
Phase Three	Fundraising: preparation for Scholastic Book Fair-make contact with sales consultant before Christmas break	10/15/09–2/01/09
	Grant writing: search funding directory. Find grants to apply for and ghost write for SUNO	10/12/09–10/16/09
	Applying for scholarships: try to help with the cost of trip to New Orleans	10/19/09–01/15/09
	Gather, document, and organize data and progress to prepare for Conference presentation	10/15/09–3/01/09
Phase Four	Scholastic Book Fair to be held in February	2/01/09–3/01/09
	Collaboration with SUNO on preparation of a presentation for library conference	
Phase Five	Delivery of materials to SUNO	3/01/09–4/01/09
	Possible presentation at SUNO	

Appendix G

Sample from the online exhibit, *IUPUI Neighborhood Project*

[http://www.ulib.iupui.edu/neighborhood/]

The 512 acre IUPUI campus continues to be an ever-growing presence in the midst of the Indianapolis downtown area. The land now occupied by the IUPUI campus was once the site of neighborhoods established from the mid-1800s to the early 1900s. Drawn by jobs in industries located along White River, native-born Hoosiers, people from other states, and immigrants from various European countries settled and formed neighborhoods near the river.

In 1824, Indianapolis became Indiana's seat of government. The city began to grow, with its population made up of immigrants from various parts of the world. German, Polish, and African American immigrants were among the first settlers to arrive. Over the course of the century, they would be followed by Irish, Jewish, and eventually even Balkan people escaping the fallen Turkish Empire. Settlers naturally tend to establish residence near a water source, so early settlers constructed dwellings and businesses along the banks of the White River.

During the 1870s concentrations of African Americans formed on what is now campus, near North and Agnes Streets (now the South side of Lockefield). By the turn of the century, the city's population had reached over 75,000, made up of immigrants from all over the world, including an especially large population of African Americans (8 percent) compared to other states at that time.

Most of the campus area's homes and businesses had become university property by the 1980s. However, there were a few

Figure AG.1 Historical map from 1930s downtown Indianapolis, Indiana

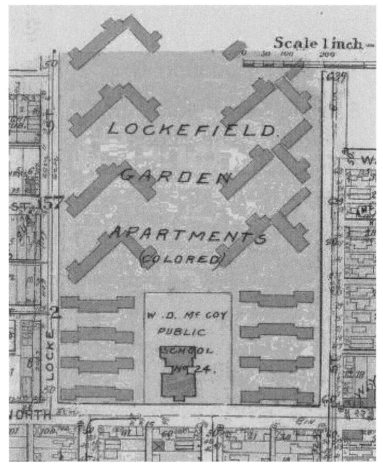

Courtesy of Indiana State Library.

people who stood their ground in the neighborhood as long as possible. Stanley Porter was the longtime owner of the building on the northeast corner of Blake and North Streets that housed his liquor store and other businesses. When approached with an option to buy his business, the owner refused to sell, describing

Figure AG.2   Image of Stanley Porter outside his store

Courtesy of IUPUI Indiana Library Special Collections and Archives.

the university's offers as enough money 'to buy a good Cadillac'. The university used eminent domain proceedings to acquire the property in 1987. The building was torn down to make way for a parking lot.

Beyond Stereotypes Instructions

Dear conversation starters,

Thank you for volunteering to participate in our brand new conversation series, 'Beyond Stereotypes!' We appreciate your cooperation and willingness to speak out about your beliefs and background. The series will be held on February 25th and 26th, from 12–2 p.m. and 4–6 p.m. on both days. The series will be advertised across campus and interested students will come to talk to you freely about the topic you have chosen to represent. We at the University Library would like to give you a short of list of ways to prepare for the series as well as what you can expect:

- Always remember to be yourself. The student will be talking to you because of your background or belief, but that is not all. We want to encourage you to share your own personal stories and help the student know exactly why you feel the way you do.

- On the flip side, if questions become too intimate or uncomfortable, you reserve the right to not answer.

- Remember that multiple students may want to talk to you, and they may have a lot of the same questions. Be prepared to answer the same questions several times.

- Keep in mind that each student wanting to talk to you will be doing so for different reasons. A good conversation starter is simply asking them why they chose you in particular to talk to!

- We would like to stress that this is a two-way discussion series. Some students may be shy and you as representatives need to be willing to carry the conversation if necessary. Suggestions include asking the student if they have ever encountered another person with your background or what their impressions are of people of your background.

- If you encounter a student who is aggressive or uncivilized in their discussion with you, make every attempt to remain calm. Try to rationally explain your stance on the topic. However, if the student continues to act out of hand, contact one of the facilitators and we will take care of the situation. Remember: **You have the right to end the discussion if you feel insulted or accused.**

- You are highly encouraged to speak with other participants throughout the series to see how their sessions are going with other students. Give each other feedback and advice; try to get the most out of this series as you can.

If you have any questions or suggestions, you can reach us at our joint e-mail address, *uldf0809@gmail.com.*

Again, we thank you sincerely for your time and look forward to working with you.

Alise and Sindhu
University Library Diversity Fellows

Date_____ Session time_____

Beyond Stereotypes: Changing Perceptions through Conversation

1. Please answer the following on a scale of 1 (not at all) to 5 (very much).

    i. Do you feel like you learned something new about a stereotype today?

        Not at all   Very much

        1   2   3   4   5

    ii. Do you feel like you learned something new about diversity today?

        Not at all   Very much

        1   2   3   4   5

    iii. Would you like to participate in a similar event in the future?

        Not at all   Very much

        1   2   3   4   5

2. What did you like most about the event? _____

    _____

3. What did you like least about the event? _____

    _____

4. Would you like the format of this event to be modified in the future?   Yes   No

    If yes, please provide some suggestions: _____

    _____

    _____

5. Please identify the role you played in the conversation series:
   □ I was a Conversation Starter
   □ I was a walk-in participant
   □ Other   Please specify:_____

Thank you for your participation!

Appendix H

Pre-proposal for the IUPUI University Library International Newsroom

Over the past two years, the IUPUI University Library's Diversity Council has undertaken several initiatives to bring diversity to the forefront of the library's operations and services. In its second year, the University Library Diversity Fellowship program gives two highly motivated IUPUI undergraduates a professional work experience in a library setting. This year-long paid opportunity offers two exceptional students a chance to collaborate with library staff on in-depth research projects, special exhibits and collection development. Also, in the spring of 2008, the library Diversity Council began providing copies of *The Indianapolis Recorder* (an historically Black local newspaper), free of charge to IUPUI students, faculty, and staff.

Positive feedback to *The Indianapolis Recorder* initiative has prompted the Diversity Council to seek to add a wider range of titles to this free newspaper program and to examine how we might make other types of foreign language news media available to students in the library. The announcement of the IUPUI Diversity Initiatives Funding opportunity allows us to broaden this diverse news program to include a variety of traditional print resources, as well as television and newsfeed outlets. The inclusion of video screens in the International Newsroom will allow the library to highlight the multimedia displays created by the library Diversity Fellows, as well as to broadcast programming from international news outlets.

University Library will consult UITS to help our Client Support and Operations Teams install televisions with cable or satellite newsfeeds from around the world. We will collaborate with the Office of International Affairs and the Journalism department in acquiring an inclusive list of newspapers and newsfeeds to represent the diversity of our student population. The Library has identified a space in its central reference area, adjacent to the Academic Commons and across from the Writing Center, as an ideal location for the new International Newsroom.

Describe the rationale of the proposal (include specifics on how it reflects Dimensions of Diversity):

University Library has several periodical subscriptions to mostly scientific publications in German and French, but few materials dealing with news and current events in those languages represented by our international students and foreign language students. This proposal would create an area of the library where a diverse population of students could access different types of media in their native languages and expose others to the diversity of cultures and languages on our campus. Currently, 3.8 percent of students at IUPUI are from the international community. A total of 132 students are enrolled in foreign language degree programs at IUPUI.

The International Newsroom will also be available to library community users. Constructed with community support, the University Library is a public library, serving the people of Indiana. Any state resident with a valid ID is eligible for a library card. Last year, we created new library accounts for more than twelve hundred community users and checked out 11,000 books to Indiana residents and high school students. Of the nearly one million visitors to the library each year, roughly 10 percent are community users.

Brief Budget Projection (maximum limit is $100,000; could be spread over 3 years):

One time Purchases:

4–5 Flat-screen Televisions	$5,000
Wiring and cable/satellite hook-up	$5,000
Newspaper Shelving 4 double wide units	
@ $680 each	$2,720

Furniture

4 1-seat chairs @ $520 each	$2,080
4 2-seat chairs @ $820 each	$3,280
4 tables 20 × 28 × 28" @ $440 each	$1,760
	Total = $19,840

Annual Purchases:
Subscriptions for the following international
newspapers @ $200 each

Chinese language newspaper (World Journal)	$200
Spanish language newspaper	$200
Japanese language newspaper	$200
Arabic language newspaper	$200
Russian language newspaper	$200
Hindi language newspaper	$200
2 African newspapers	$400
Satellite or cable television service	$1,200
	Total = $2,800

Do you have the endorsement of Dean's and/or Vice Chancellor's heads?

David Lewis, Dean of the University Library, has endorsed the plan for an International Newsroom in the library and he has committed to funding subscriptions and resources for the project on an annual basis going forward in the amount of $5,000.

Application
President's University Diversity Initiative

Office of the Vice President for Diversity, Equity, and Multicultural Affairs

Applying unit:

☐ Academic ☐ Administrative √ Support ☐ Other (specify): _____

Primary Contact Information:

Name: University Library Diversity Council

E-mail: in-ulib-diversity@exchange.iu.edu

Unit: University Library

Campus: IUPUI

Total Funds Requested: $100,000

Project Period: initial installation 5 mos./ongoing

Diversity Dimension(s) to be addressed:

☐ Institutional Leadership and Commitment

√ Curricular and Co-Curricular Transformation

√ Campus Climate

☐ Representational Diversity

Purpose Statement:

Please give a short overview of how you plan to use the funding and what you expect to accomplish with the funds. What are the overall goals for your project?

The IUPUI University Library will create an International Newsroom by repurposing existing space in its Reference Room, the highest traffic area in the library, close to the Reference Desk, University Writing Center, and the Academic Commons. The name 'International Newsroom' illustrates that news crosses all borders, not just cultural and lingual, but geopolitical boundaries as well. The Newsroom will bring a diverse collection of international and alternative news resources to IUPUI students, faculty, and staff via print newspapers and publications and satellite television programming (with closed captioning whenever available) in a number of languages. Traditional print and broadcast media will be utilized alongside newer technology, such as blogs, podcasts, and RSS feeds, available via designated kiosks. The space will contain soft seating and tables and chairs that can be easily moved so users can reconfigure the space to their needs. Local print newspapers will be purchased in quantity by University Library, permitting students to take free copies for personal use. (University Library currently has such an arrangement with *The Indianapolis Recorder*, the well-known local African American weekly newspaper.)

The International Newsroom will also be available to the local Central Indiana community. Of the nearly one million visitors to University Library each year, approximately 10 percent are community users. Last year, we created new library accounts for more than 1,200 community users and checked out 11,000 books to Indiana residents and high school students.

The University Library Diversity Council will seek input from the IUPUI Office of International Affairs, IU School of Journalism, Department of World Languages and Cultures (via librarian liaison), the new Multicultural Center, and community partners to develop an inclusive collection that will best represent our students and local community. News resources identified to date represent perspectives from China/Taiwan, India, Saudi Arabia, Nigeria, and the Latino/Hispanic, GLBT, and homeless communities.

University Library has long had an embedded librarian in the Center for Teaching and Learning who can work with CTL staff to introduce faculty to the International Newsroom. They can suggest ways faculty can use the space and its resources in their courses, such as reading a specific blog as part of an assignment or by bringing small groups to the Newsroom to view a broadcast. We plan to approach University College as well to determine if the International Newsroom may be utilized to support diversity initiatives and the Campus Common Theme for freshman learning communities.

University Library's Client Support and Operations Teams will collaborate with UITS to install and maintain televisions with international news feeds via cable or satellite. The Client Support and Operations Teams will install and maintain the computer kiosks.

Overall Goals

- Establish a comfortable and secure space in which our increasing number of international students will find news and current events from and about their own countries in their native languages (currently, 3.8 percent of students at IUPUI are from the international community). This may provide a sense of belonging for international as well as minority students and faculty.
- Provide a place where all students can be exposed to different languages and new cultures or viewpoints in a variety of learning style formats.
- Present additional ways for faculty to expose students to diverse cultures and points of view as a means of incorporating the Principles of Undergraduate Learning, particularly 'Understanding Society and Culture' and 'Critical Thinking'.

Detailed Plan:

Goal: Broaden campus community's worldview and increase exposure to international and alternative news sources through the creation of an International Newsroom on second floor of University Library.				
Measurable Objective	Key Action Steps/Activities	Expected Outcome	Budget Resources Required	Timeline for Completion
Provide in-building access to 7–10 foreign newspapers	Identify and order newspapers representative of IUPUI's international student population in the native language if applicable	7–10 foreign newspapers start arriving at the library	■ $5,000 a year for 3 years	■ All orders placed by 1 month from award receipt ■ Newspapers start arriving about 2 months from award receipt
Provide multiple copies of 4–5 locally published alternative/ minority newspapers for patrons to take home with them	Identify and place orders for multiple copies of locally published alternative/ minority newspapers representative IUPUI and Indianapolis community	Copies of locally published newspapers start arriving at the library	■ $2,100 a year for 3 years	■ All orders placed by 1 month from award of money ■ Newspapers start arriving about 2 months from award receipt

Provide comfortable and convenient space for utilizing the newsroom resources	1) Remove furniture 2) Purchase and install new furniture	International Newsroom is furnished except for electronics	■ $1,000 for moving ■ $16,300 for new furniture	■ Place orders within 1 month of award receipt ■ Furniture installed within 3 months of award receipt
Provide access to 4 international satellite news broadcasts	1) Purchase video and audio equipment 2) Install video and audio equipment	International Newsroom has TVs with satellite connections to international TV broadcasts	■ Annual cost for news subscriptions $11,533 a year for 3 years totaling $34,600 ■ Video hardware $18,600	■ Access to international news broadcasts available to IUPUI and Indianapolis community 5 months after award receipt
Provide access to a variety of international and alternative internet news sources such as blogs, rss feeds, podcasts, etc.	1) Purchase 4 computer workstations 2) Hire webmaster to develop International Newsroom presence	International Newsroom has web presence which provides access to a variety of online news sources	■ 4 computer workstations $4,100 ■ Compensation for webmaster, $10 an hour for about 90 hours to set up and maintain web portal, $900	■ Website running 3 months after award receipt

Sustainability:

Please specify how your unit/campus will sustain the proposed initiative(s) after the project award period.

> This award will allow University Library to make the necessary changes to existing space and purchase the hardware necessary to establish this space. Subscriptions to well-utilized news resources will become a line item in the University Library budget with support provided by collection development funds. Unpopular or underutilized resources (determined by tracking usage statistics) will be removed and possibly replaced.

Detailed Budget Narrative:

Please provide a detailed narrative justifying the anticipated use of the requested funds for each year of the project period.

In order to create the International Newsroom, we will hire Stuarts Moving and Storage to remove the existing cabinets and furniture from the area at a cost of $1,000. Side tables, seating for sixteen, a computer kiosk with chairs and shelving units for newspapers will be installed at an estimated cost of $16,300. Four computers will be housed in the kiosk, at a total cost of $4,100. The Newsroom will have four mounted televisions for viewing international newsfeeds installed at a total cost of $5,600. An estimate from SCOLA on hardware (DVR, C-Band, reflector, AZ/EL mount, cable, and assorted tools) needed to provide international news programming is approximating $13,000. An additional $3,200 is required to purchase FM transmitters and receivers for audio feed.

With the furniture and hardware in place, we will then subscribe to the resources to be included in the International Newsroom. SCOLA's annual subscription fee for six channels of programming is approximately $11,533, for a total of $34,600 over the three years. Subscriptions to local alternative and international newspapers will cost approximately $7,100 annually and allowing for anticipated subscription rate inflation over time. Users will also be able to access blogs and podcasts from the computer kiosks in the International Newsroom. A webmaster will be compensated $10 per hour for 90 hours to set up and maintain the web portal.

Provost/Chancellor Approval:

Signed: _____   Date: _____

Appendix I

International Reading Room and International News Sources

Name _____

You will spend 5–8 minutes at three stations in the International Newsroom viewing news broadcasts from around the world. You will be in groups of no more than 5 at each station. Please complete the required information for each of the stations.

1st International News Station
TV Station: _____
Country/Countries Covered: _____

Observations of the news: what type of news was covered? (Even if the broadcast is not in English, what did you notice?) How was the presentation similar to news in the United States? How was the presentation different from news in the United States? Consider the set, the news presenter, visuals, etc.

_____
_____
_____
_____
_____
_____

2nd International News Station
TV Station: _____
Country/Countries Covered: _____

Observations of the news: what type of news was covered? (Even if the broadcast is not in English, what did you notice?) How was the presentation similar to news in the United States? How was the presentation different from news in the United States? Consider the set, the news presenter, visuals, etc.

_____

_____

_____

_____

_____

_____

3rd International News Station

TV Station: _____

Country/Countries Covered: _____

Observations of the news: what type of news was covered? (Even if the broadcast is not in English, what did you notice?) How was the presentation similar to news in the United States? How was the presentation different from news in the United States? Consider the set, the news presenter, visuals, etc.

_____

_____

_____

_____

_____

International News Sources
1. Write down 3 helpful hints for accessing news from non-US sources.

2. What information should you capture (write down) when you use information from a website?

Write down three sources (databases, websites, journals, etc.) where you can find information about your country and WHY this site is helpful (what type of information can be found).

1.

2.

3.

Appendix J

International Reading Room
and International News Sources
September 3, 2009

Name _____

You will spend 10 minutes at three stations in the International Newsroom viewing news broadcasts from around the world. You will be in groups of no more than 5 at each station. Please complete the required information for each of the stations. Be sure to focus on what you see and interpret.

1st International News Station
TV Station: _____
Country/Countries Covered: _____

Observations of the news: what did you observe about the presenters? What topics were covered based on images, video and other visuals? How does this differ with what you've seen on news in Indiana or other parts of the United States? Where the topics similar? Where the topics different?

_____
_____
_____
_____
_____
_____

2nd International News Station
TV Station: _____
Country/Countries Covered: _____

Observations of the news: what did you observe about the presenters? What topics were covered based on images, video and other visuals? How does this differ with what you've seen on news in Indiana or other parts of the United States? Where the topics similar? Where the topics different?

_____

_____

_____

_____

_____

_____

3rd International News Station
TV Station: _____
Country/Countries Covered: _____

Observations of the news: what did you observe about the presenters? What topics were covered based on images, video and other visuals? How does this differ with what you've seen on news in Indiana or other parts of the United States? Where the topics similar? Where the topics different?

_____

_____

_____

_____

_____

_____

International News Sources
1. Write down 3 helpful hints for accessing news from non-US sources.

2. What information should you capture (write down) when you use information from a website?

Write down three sources (databases, websites, journals, etc.) where you can find information about your country and WHY this site is helpful (what type of information can be found).
1.

2.

3.

Selected Bibliography

Aguiñaga, J.A. (1999) International perspective – view of the concept of diversity in other countries. *Journal of Library Administration*, 27(1), 171–90.

Alire, C.A. (2007) Word-of-mouth marketing: abandoning the academic library ivory tower. *New Library World*, 108, 545–51.

Altbach, P. G. (2000) The crisis in multinational higher education. *Change*, 32(6), 28–31.

Bartell, M. (2003) Internationalization of universities: a university culture-based framework. *Higher Education*, 45(1), 43–70.

Calvert, P. (2001) International variations in measuring customer expectations. *Library Trends*, 49, 732–57.

Cheung, H.Y. and Chan, A.W. (2010) Education and competitive economy: how do cultural dimensions fit in? *Higher Education*, 59, 525–41.

Crossman, J. and Clarke, M. (2010) International experience and graduate employability: stakeholder perceptions on the connection. *Higher Education*, 59, 599–613.

Dewey, B.I. and Parham, L., (ed.) (2006) *Achieving diversity*. New York: Neal-Schuman.

Drago, W.A. and Wagner, R.J. (2004) Vark preferred learning styles and online education. *Management research news*, 27(7), 1–13.

Elicker, J., Thompson, M., Snell, A. and O'Malley, A. (2009) A training framework and follow-up observations for multiculturally inclusive teaching: is believing that we are emphasizing diversity enough? *Journal of diversity in higher education*, 2(2), 63–77.

Fabian, C.A., D'aniello, C., Tysick, C. and Morin, M. (2004) Multiple models for library outreach initiatives. *Reference Librarian*, 39(82), 39–55.

Friday, A. (2002) Holistic approach to diversity: practical projects for promoting inclusivity. In M.C. Kelly (ed.) *Making the grade:*

academic libraries and student success (pp. 17–36). Chicago: Association of College and Research Libraries.

Hollingsworth, J. (2009) University library's undergraduate diversity fellowship. *Indiana Libraries*, 28(2), 2–6.

Horta, H. (2009) Global and national prominent universities: internationalization, competitiveness and the role of the State. *Higher Education*, 58, 387–405.

Hover, P.L. and Lu, J. (2009) 'Sentences like these': multicultural information dynamics and international diversity of thought. *International Information & Library Review*, 41, 196–218.

Kathman, J.M. and Kathman, M.D. (1998) What difference does diversity make in managing student employees? *College & research libraries*, 59(4), 378–89.

Lee, W.O. (2008) Repositioning of high education from its expanded visions: lifelong learning, entrepreneurship, internationalization and integration. *Education Research Policy and Practice*, 7, 73–83.

Love, E. (2009) Simple step: integrating library reference and instruction into previously established academic programs for minority students. *Reference librarian*, 50, 4–13.

Love, J.B. (2001) Assessment of diversity initiatives in academic libraries. *Journal of library administration*, 33(1), 73–103.

Martin, C.K., Maxy-Harris, C., Graybill, J.O. and Rodacker-Borgens, E.K. (2009) Closing the gap: investigating the search skills of international and U.S. students: An exploratory study. *Library philosophy and practice*, 11(2). Retrieved from *http://unllib.unl.edu/LPP/martin-maxeyharris-graybill-rodackerborgens.pdf*

Martin, R.R. (1994) *Libraries and the changing face of academia.* Metuchen, NJ: Scarecrow Pr.

Mestre, L. (2010) *Librarians serving diverse populations: challenges and opportunities.* Chicago: Association of College and Research Libraries.

Mu, C. (2007) Marketing academic library resources and information services to international students from Asia. *Reference services review*, 35, 571–83.

Mundava, M.C. and Gray, L. (2008) Meeting them where they are: Marketing to international student populations in U.S. academic libraries. *Technical Services Quarterly*, 25(3), 35–48.

Osborne, N.S. and Poon, C. (1995) Servicing diverse library populations through the specialized instructional services concept. *The Reference Librarian*, 51, 285–94.

Puente, M.A., Gray, L. and Agnew, S. (2009) Expanding the library wall: outreach to the University of Tennessee's multicultural/ international student population. *Reference services review*, 37(1), 30–43.

Rivza, B. and Teichler, U. (2007) Changing role of student mobility. *Higher education policy*, 20, 457–75.

Royse, M., Conner, T. and Miller, T. (2006) Charting a course for diversity: An experience in climate assessment. *Portal: libraries and the academy*, 6 (1), 23–45.

Sciame-Giesecke, S., Roden, D. and Parkison, K. (2009) Infusing diversity into the curriculum: what are faculty members actually doing? *Journal of diversity in higher education*, 2(3), 156–65.

Simmons-Welburn, J. (1999) Diversity dialogue groups: a model for enhancing work place diversity. *Journal of library administration*, 27(1), 111–21.

Simmons-Welburn, J. and Welburn, W.C. (2001) Cultivating partnerships/realizing diversity. *Journal of library administration*, 33(1), 5–19.

Stanley, M.J. (2007) Case study: where is the diversity? Focus groups on how students view the face of librarianship. *Library administration & mangement*, 21 (2), 83–9.

Summers, M. and Volet, S. (2008) Students' attitudes towards culturally mixed groups on international campuses: impact of participation in diverse and non-diverse groups. *Studies in higher education*, 33, 357–70.

Switzer, A.T. (2008) Redefining diversity: creating an inclusive academic library through diversity initiatives. *College & undergraduate libraries*, 15, 280–300.

Tucker, T. (2009) Partnerships beyond the university campus: community connections that work. In N. Courtney (ed.) *Academic library outreach*. Westport, CT: Libraries Unlimited.

Van der Wende, M.C. (2001) Internationalisation policies: About new trends and contrasting paradigms. *Higher education policy*, 14, 249–59.

Walter, S. (2005) Moving beyond collections: academic library outreach to multicultural student centers. *Reference Services Review*, 33, 438–58.

Wang, J. and Frank, D. (2002) Cross-cultural communication: Implications for effective information services in academic libraries. *portal: Libraries and the Academy*, 2, 207–16.

Welch, A. R. (1997) The peripatetic professor: The internationalisation of the academic profession. *Higher Education*, 34, 323–45.

Whitmire, E. (2003) Cultural diversity and undergraduates' academic library use. *Journal of Academic Librarianship*, 29(3), 148–62.

Winston, M. and Li, H. (2000) Managing diversity in liberal arts college libraries. *College & Research Libraries*, 61(3), 205–15.

Yang, Z.Y. and White, B. (2007) Evaluation of a diversity program at an academic library. *Library Philosophy and Practice.* Retrieved from *http://www.webpages.uidaho.edu/~mbolin/ yang.pdf*

Young, C. (2006) Collection development and diversity on CIC academic library web sites. *Journal of Academic Librarianship*, 32, 370–6.

Index

CPSIA information can be obtained at www.ICGtesting.com
Printed in the USA
BVOW06s2121131215

430161BV00003B/36/P

9 781843 346357